Dr. Jensen's
GUIDE TO NATURAL
WEIGHT CONTROL

Dr. Jensen's
GUIDE TO NATURAL
WEIGHT CONTROL
A BALANCED APPROACH
TO WELL-BEING

Bernard Jensen, D.C., Ph.D.
Clinical Nutritionist

KEATS PUBLISHING

LOS ANGELES

NTC/Contemporary Publishing Group

The purpose of this book is to educate. It is sold with the understanding that the publisher and author shall have neither liability nor
responsibility for any injury caused or alleged to be caused directly or
indirectly by the information contained in this book. While every
effort has been made to ensure its accuracy, the book's contents
should not be construed as medical advice. Each person's health needs
are unique. To obtain recommendations appropriate to your particular
situation, please consult a qualified health-care provider.

Library of Congress Cataloging-in-Publication Data

Jensen, Bernard, 1908–
    Dr. Jensen's guide to natural weight control / Bernard Jensen.
      p. cm.
    Includes index.
    ISBN 0-658-00276-7
    1. Weight loss. 2. Health. 3. Nutrition. I. Title: Doctor Jensen's
guide to natural weight control. II. Title: Guide to natural weight
control. III. Title.

RM222.2 .J475 2000
613.7—dc21   00-038460

Design by Andrea Reider

Published by Keats Publishing
A division of NTC/Contemporary Publishing Group, Inc.
4255 West Touhy Avenue, Lincolnwood, Illinois 60712, U.S.A.

Printed and bound in the United States of America
International Standard Book Number: 0-658-00276-7
   01 02 03 04 VP 18 17 16 15 14 13 12 11 10 9 8 7 6 5 4 3 2

CONTENTS

FOREWORD

As I see it, overweight equals a state of dishar-mony, a sign that we haven't come into our real selves. At my health ranch, I treat obesity as if it were a symptom of disease because it is always either rooted in a lifestyle problem, a self-image issue, or a physical dysfunction. It is always caused by something. In fact, many times obesity may either be caused by a disease or, conversely, may itself con-tribute to a disease and be linked to a host of potential prob-lems in the body.

We find that a disease can result in a poor metabolism so that we cannot break down the fat we ingest. The liver can be at fault. The pancreas can be underfunctioning, not taking care of the starches and sugars. There is a possibility we are not get-ting enough oxygen. An underactive thyroid can be responsi-ble in this case. The circulation can be poor.

Possibly it comes back to simple things such as the kitchen table being responsible for an overweight condition. It may be that our environment isn't good. Pollution can cause trouble, especially when fumes, gases, odors, and so forth affect the thy-roid gland and trigger imbalance in the metabolism, producing a lack of oxygenation. Of course, oxygenation is needed for burning up the fatty tissue in the body. We have to look at the diet; we have to look at the lifestyle; we have to look at the mentality and attitude; we have to look at diseases that may be contributing to obesity or being overweight. So we have many things to consider. This is why we have to look at obesity as a disease.

Obesity contributes to the malfunctioning of the human body in a myriad of ways. They include physiological symptoms such as high blood pressure, atherosclerosis, arteriosclerosis, diabetes, and venous congestion. In addition, however, there are many indirect physical and psychological impacts upon the person carrying too many excess pounds. The obese person may be a well-nourished person, but most often it is unchecked preferences for high-calorie, low-nutrition foods, or a poorly balanced diet that have contributed to this state. This calorie-stuffed, vitamin-and-mineral deficient individual is rarely a happy person. Not only does the person's own self-esteem suffer from the knowledge that his or her potential is going unattained, but there is also great external pressure from a society that places increasing emphasis on looking and acting trim, fit, and youthful.

I cannot promise eternal youth, of course, but I can offer a new vitality, increased energy, and the joy of a better-functioning body at its correct weight to anyone who is willing to read carefully, to take me seriously, and to exercise the self-control required to break old habits and establish a new healthful lifestyle. Happily, the "willpower" phase is relatively brief—again and again my patients report that as they begin to treat their bodies kindly with proper nutrition and exercise, they no longer crave the foods that formerly were their downfall.

In this book, my goal is to give you some basic concepts of nutrition, exercise, and overall good health, plus the motivation to apply this knowledge at home. According to studies done by various universities, at least 55 percent of the people in the United States qualify as overweight or obese (normally defined as having a body mass index [BMI] greater than 30, or about 30 pounds overweight). The BMI is based on body weight relative to height, and overweight, by this standard, is usually 20 percent over the norm for a person's height. Impersonal statistics aside, the one great need I see is that I must take care of the patient on the other end of the symptoms.

Now, of course, it is sometimes very difficult to teach a person to watch calories carefully and exercise regularly. I would say that 70 percent of the patients who are overweight need to learn these things. This is where this book is really going to be of value to the average person.

The average person should recognize that we cannot solve the basic problem of being overweight with drugs or surgery. There are all kinds of doctoring methods applied today to overcoming obesity. Often people take pills because they want to go the easiest way. One of my patients was a doctor who wanted to reduce weight without changing his habits of living. He weighed almost 250 pounds, and he told me, "I'll wait until they make food out of sawdust so I won't gain any weight." Well, he is still waiting, which is pure procrastination.

If we look at being overweight as a chronic disease or condition, we find it develops little by little because the patient transgresses certain natural laws. For instance, eating more calories than you use each day results in continuous weight gain. In this book, we're trying to get you to see such laws from a dietary standpoint, even from a psychological standpoint. We find that the psychologist today does a lot of good work just by taking care of the mind of a person, and losing weight is both a mental and physical exercise. On the mental side, we have to consider the home environment, the family situation and relationships, and the person's attitude. What cultural or other learned food preferences does this person have? How much change is this person willing to make for the sake of becoming slender and energetic?

Because most people gain weight pleasurably at the table, they have not been prodded to seek professional help because of pains, aches, or other usual symptoms of dysfunction. The pounds creep on, almost unnoticed, until, one day, you realize there are no notches left to let out your belt, your clothes have all "shrunk" beyond wearability, you're too tired and too short of breath to really enjoy the exercise you know you need, and the road back to slenderness begins to look long indeed.

On the physical side, we have to consider diet, body chemistry, circulation, and exercise. Above all, I would say that 70 percent of the potential for successful weight control depends on the patient's attitude toward this process. It is impossible to give a patient a pill, a "magic bullet" for a fast cure. You worked your way into this trouble, as a rule, and you will have to work your way out of it. As you return to a natural weight, you will go through an adjustment period, and this is not always pleasant. We have to consider that such an adjustment period may occur.

But there is hope. As far as testimonials are concerned, I could tell you about Dolly Dimple of circus fame, who once weighed 555 pounds. After following my reducing diet, she weighed only 118 pounds, and she stayed there. I can tell you about our own office employees who took hold of some of these ideas. One young woman lost 50 pounds and another lost 20 pounds. I see this sort of thing happening often enough to be extremely encouraged.

I want to encourage you to follow a good philosophy for handling your life. Without a good philosophy, you cannot be slender. You may find problems in your work. You may find problems in your marriage. You may find your lifestyle produces stress and strain. Each of these may be contributing to your overeating. You need a philosophy that guides you, one that is going to help you with these things.

This book is put together with the idea that the best path for the most people is the middle way. I have tried to show you what to watch out for. I have tried to tell you that successful weight-loss dieting requires patience and persistence. I recommend that you stay on the healthy side as much as possible.

When you succeed in losing weight with a good reducing diet, then you should follow it up with a healthy way of living to keep your weight down. You should know that most reducing diets are not complete. They cannot build a whole body because they are one-sided diets, lacking in the balance of nutrients we need. My diet is balanced to meet all nutritional needs while you are losing weight, and I introduce exercise plans and many lifestyle tips to maintain a healthy way of life during and after your weight loss goal is reached.

There are specific people who need supervision. It doesn't work for everyone just to go off on his own. Some dieting measures are harmful, and you have to make sure you are not following a dangerous diet. Sometimes overcoming the results of extreme diets is a very difficult journey. We know those people who suffer from anorexia nervosa and bulimia are difficult to handle. Sometimes it is best to have the supervision and experience of a doctor who has handled these kinds of

cases. I urge anyone with a health condition to consult a doctor before beginning this or any diet and exercise program.
Certain conditions may be aggravated by even a well-balanced
nutritional program.

Resolving your weight problem is a way of enlightenment
if you follow the path presented in this book. You will feel
good, look good, and, more important, you'll be motivated
enough by the way you look and feel to stay on the path of
harmony, the path of health, the path of right living. You can
tell yourself that this is the diet you've always been looking for.

Caiman Canada
www.Caiman.ca

Hello,

Please find enclosed order

058-4014870-0281360 from 6/29/2008

Enjoy!

However, should you encounter any problems with it, don't hesitate to contact us at canada@caiman.com .

Thank you for having ordered with Caiman Canada .

Sincerely,

Caiman Canada

Qty	Item Description
1	Dr. Jensen's Guide to Natural Weight Control [Paperback] by Jensen, Bernard

Thanks for shopping at Caiman Canada, and please come again!

INTRODUCTION

There are so many books, pills, and powders on the market these days that promise quick and easy weight loss that the average person tends to be confused about the right way to lose excess weight. In over sixty years of sanitarium practice, I have helped hundreds of overweight men and women grow slender without drugs or reducing powders, and this was accomplished without actually focusing on weight reduction. How? By introducing them to a more natural way of living.

The key to weight control is not dieting but *lifestyle*. Nutrition, exercise, rest, fresh air, sunshine, recreation, work, and relationships all affect our state of well-being, and our body weight molds to those things. When I teach a patient how to change to a healthier, more natural lifestyle, and the patient follows my program faithfully, body weight normalizes. That is, overweight persons tend to lose weight, while underweight persons tend to gain. We find that nature knows best, but sometimes we have to give her a helping hand.

Most people do not realize that a balanced weight control program must be learned, just as we would learn to play the piano. During the first few practice sessions, we can expect to hit a few sour notes. It is normal to make mistakes in learning a new skill, and we must come to realize that mistakes are not evidence of failure but signs that we need to keep practicing. Practice makes perfect, they say.

There are many salient points about food habits that I will be taking up in this book. We will be discussing the fact that when life is not going the way we think it should, when we have an unpleasant job, an unpleasant marriage, or a loveless life, we often turn to eating as a crutch. This is not the way to live. Eating should be a happy, pleasurable process, but it shouldn't be a substitute for something that isn't going right in our lives. We need to solve the problems that tend to alter our food habits, and get on with the business of life.

When we use a balanced, high-fiber food regimen to lose weight, we are giving our bodies the utmost support in meeting nutritional needs while taking off excess pounds. By the time you finish reading this book, you will understand why so many weight-loss diets invite rebound weight gain after dieting is over, and why mine does not. You will learn how the body and mind readjust to weight changes and to changes in food intake, and how nature's reversal process will not only help you reduce but give you greater vitality and energy.

I don't believe that an unnatural diet plan or reducing program will help you reach and stay at your natural weight. The overwhelming evidence from many research studies is that 95 percent of those who go on crash diets regain all or more than their old weight within one year. That's nearly everyone who diets! Researchers may yet come up with an effective, relatively permanent weight control plan, but I feel that we can't top nature. Our bodies and minds are made to conform to certain natural laws and principles, and it is by staying within those laws and principles that we feel and look our best. This is what I have taught for over fifty years. This is what has brought the best results for my patients.

The program presented in this book is aimed at mature adults who are willing to use willpower to practice living right until they are living right and not just practicing.

One of the simplest and most effective diet procedures I know is to take a normal helping of good wholesome food at mealtime, then separate one-third to one-half of each food item off to the side of the plate and eat only the rest. This can also be varied by the amount of exercise you do.

Just as fat develops from eating more food than we expend in energy, its loss depends on eating less than we expend in energy. This is the reversal process well known to those familiar with the body's natural means of getting rid of disease. The wonderful thing about my weight-loss diet is that our bodies adjust well to this program, so we don't experience the extreme sense of deprivation during the diet or the rebound weight gain afterward. I realize that you can lose weight faster with drugs, extreme exercise, imbalanced diets, fasting, and other available methods, but my way is one of the safest and best ways to go. I feel that nature's way is best, but sometimes we need to help her out with a little common sense.

The two greatest exercises I know for reducing are shaking the head from side to side at food and pushing yourself away from the table before you are full. This is the way to discover a new "you," a slimmer, healthier you. Discipline is one of the keys.

In this book, however, I have tried to make losing weight more attractive, interesting, and motivating than it would be if you relied totally on self-discipline. My thirty-day diet plan, on page 186, includes sufficient variety in foods to please almost anyone, and it is consistent in its nutritional value and calorie content with the most up-to-date, reliable research on weight reduction. I feel that it is a diet plan anyone can follow.

Anyone over forty years of age, more than 10 pounds over-weight, or with any chronic disease should discuss this pro-gram with her doctor before trying it. Conditions such as diabetes, hypoglycemia, and heart disease can be greatly aggra-vated by a reducing diet.

WE ARE WHAT WE DIGEST

Many times I have said, *"It is not what we eat that counts but what we digest."* If the digestion is poor, we are not getting all of the good from our foods, no matter how careful we are about selecting and preparing the most nourishing foods. We may have to take digestive supplements as found in health food stores to aid digestion. Poor digestion may be a factor in weight problems, and a good digestant can be of help.

How we conduct ourselves at the table has an effect on digestion. In past years, participants in the Olympic Games were not allowed by their coaches to discuss anything of a negative or controversial nature at the table. Why? Because digestion is impaired by such conversation, and performance is affected adversely. The table is no place for accusation, argu-ment, gossip, bad news, or the disciplining of children. Leave work problems at work; don't bring them to the dinner table. Talk should be light, uplifting, humorous, and inspiring.

Champion athletes tend to avoid fried foods, cold foods, greasy foods, and having liquids with meals. This is part of their program for staying as fit as possible, and we should follow their example. One recent study showed that Americans eat twice as much fat as they should. In the United States, the average person's food habits are faulty to the extreme. We need to change.

WALKING AND SWIMMING ARE HEALTHY AND THINNING

President Harry S Truman set a wonderful exercise example for the nation by walking to work at the White House every day. And when I say walking, I mean vigorous walking, swinging the arms, and taking long, fast strides. This is what we have to do to exercise the heart, move the blood, tone the muscles, and burn away the fat. Swimming is just as good as walking and much better for those who have back problems. We have to burn off calories, besides not eating them, to make a change. Half an hour of vigorous exercise raises the metabolic rate for nearly fifteen hours afterward, burning calories the whole time. Exercise brings faster results in any reducing program.

Any exercise is good if it isn't too strenuous for your age and physical condition. To get the best results, however, you must exercise regularly at least five days a week.

BE GOOD TO YOURSELF!

How do you respond when someone gives you a compliment? Most of us like to get compliments from others, and even like to give them, but many people don't know how to be good to themselves. It is not difficult for an overweight person to develop low self-esteem and to begin thinking negatively about himself. This brings no benefit to anyone.

To begin a healthy lifestyle, start by looking on the bright side. Accept your body. Like yourself. You are unique, and there is no one else quite like you on the whole planet. There are things only you can do. If you need a regular program to break out of a low self-esteem pattern, then get up ten minutes earlier every morning to change it. When people feel neglected, are hungry for approval and affection, or are lacking the love they feel they need, they often turn to calories, especially sweets. This can be changed.

Don't be afraid to say silly things like, "I appreciate myself. I accept my body and am learning to love it. I am thankful for my gifts and talents." When you pass a mirror or stand in front of one, smile and practice liking yourself. Say, "I have the power to decide how I am going to live my life." Be sure to say it out loud.

Sometimes people think of snacking or overeating as a way of rewarding themselves. There are many better ways you can be good to yourself besides eating. Select alternatives, such as taking a nice walk, going shopping, or getting involved with a hobby.

THE HOLISTIC VIEW

Our emphasis, in taking the holistic approach, is not to treat the *symptoms* of being overweight but to take care of the *whole person* on the other end of those symptoms. Then the weight will generally normalize.

I don't like to bring religion into this, but I have to say that for many persons, the problem of being overweight could have a spiritual basis. There are certain universal spiritual laws we should keep to reach our fullest life potential, such as *Love thy neighbor as thyself,* and *Forgive those who spitefully use you.* Carrying a sense of guilt, shame, or low self-image may contribute to excess weight. We must learn to release these things, and that is a spiritual issue. Spiritual laws are not optional. They must be followed to get the best out of life. We all have our lessons to learn, and the purpose of spiritual laws is to show us what our full potentials are in life.

At the mental or psychological level, there are many reasons why people become overweight. One of my patients would overeat because he feared never getting enough food. Others snacked when they were bored or depressed, and they seemed to be bored or depressed quite often. We have to honestly confront and admit to ourselves why we overeat, and in chapter 4, I present a list of questions to help you become more aware of why and when you overeat.

Physically, there are a variety of causes of excess weight. Glandular imbalance is one. Inherited genetic traits may influence weight. Diabetes may stimulate excess weight gain or may be a result of improper food habits. Poor diet, faulty digestion, or imbalanced assimilation can cause weight gain. Sedentary jobs, chronic depression, and parental modeling influence weight. The most common cause of excess weight is habitual overeating, pure and simple, and the next cause is lack of sufficient exercise.

Losing weight is simple but not easy. You can, however, make any weight-loss program much easier to follow if you muster up willpower, courage, imagination, resolve, and a sincere desire to change to a way of life that is specifically suited for you. That is, coordinate all spiritual, mental, and physical resources to achieve your goal of finding and keeping a healthy lifestyle. Write down weight-loss goals and work for them. You will get there. You can overcome any problem in which your own choices and decisions are the key to its solution.

Most animals in their natural environments are lithe and slim with bright eyes, glossy coats, quick reflexes, and strong muscles. They live very close to the vegetable kingdom in the foods they eat. Most animals stay trim on fresh fruits, vegetables, seeds, grasses, and so forth. The predators eat fresh meat unadulterated by hormones or antibiotics, and they eat the organ meats first, which are rich in vitamins, minerals, and high-quality protein. Animals in nature eat whole, pure, natural foods, and they get plenty of exercise as they search for their food.

Man dries, cans, and preserves his fruits in sugar and chemical additives, refines his sugar and flour, and packages many refined foods so that they are high in calories and low in food value. Processing and refining white flour removes all bran and fiber and all or most of the twenty-five of the forty-four essential vitamins and minerals. Many prepared foods today have more calories than the body was designed to use. If we stay with the whole, pure, natural foods, we will be getting more nutritional value and fewer calories.

All diets are made up of protein, carbohydrates, and fats from meat, fish, poultry, dairy products, fruit, vegetables, grains, seeds, nuts, and legumes. The diet in chapter 9 is especially balanced with selections of these foods in proportions recommended by the National Academy of Sciences but conforming closely to nature's principles of whole, pure, and natural. Keep in mind that a diet can have the *proportions* right and the *calories* right but can still be *wrong* for your body. There is a great deal of difference between a pound of sugar (1,739 calories) and a pound of spinach (113 calories), despite the fact that both are carbohydrates. Spinach is high in food value; sugar is not.

In chapter 9, we present charts of approved foods as close to natural, whole, and pure as possible, with the calories they represent. This will make it easier for you to stay healthy as you lose weight.

I strongly recommend that you see a doctor before going on this or any diet to make sure that physical problems are not responsible for your being overweight. I have found certain lab tests helpful in determining any special nutritional needs to be considered while you are dieting. It is useful for overweight persons to have a thyroid test, and I also recommend what is called the SMA Panel, a complete blood analysis, and a urinalysis. These tests help reveal glandular imbalance, possible anemia, low mineral levels, kidney problems, and other potential trouble areas. Anemia, for example, can make weight reduction very difficult; it should be taken care of before beginning my weight-reduction plan. Talk to your doctor about any additional laboratory tests that might be helpful. Most deficiencies will be taken care of by the Health and Harmony Food Regimen.

In this book, I am sharing the knowledge you'll need to succeed in losing weight and staying fit. These are things you need to know, and I urge you to read slowly, thoughtfully, and carefully. It has taken me fifty years to find out and confirm much of the information presented here, and it will be very useful to you.

Impatience, as you will find, is one of the worst enemies of weight-loss dieting and has proven to be self-defeating, while the best friend of slenderizing is a positive outlook, one of confidence and expectation of good results.

THE WINNING ATTITUDE

I believe all you need to be able to lose the weight you want to lose is the right knowledge and the knowledge that you are doing the right thing. Part of what we teach is how to have a winning attitude.

Through the first part of the book, you will acquire knowledge; then you will be equipped to put our Thirty-Day Diet Plan to work. Go into this process knowing it is going to work for you, knowing that you will be able to shape up and have the body you want. We are leaving the diet plan until last so you will be ready and eager to put it to work.

I realize there are some harsh facts in this book, but we need to know these things and realize that none of us is perfect. Learn from them, but don't be disturbed by them. Take life one step at a time.

Everyone appreciates a gift they earn through effort and perseverance. Perhaps the most valuable gift you will ever give yourself is a "new you"! Good health and the sense of well-being that goes with it are seldom experienced without intentional application of effort and self-discipline.

CHAPTER 1

ARE YOU AN OBESITY STATISTIC?

A recent survey showed that 55 percent of all Americans are overweight, 22 percent of them falling into the category of obese. Obesity is assessed on the basis of three factors: having a body mass index (BMI) of 30 or more, waist circumference, and a person's risk factors for disease and conditions related to obesity. In the *Ten State Nutrition Survey*, 25 percent of adult men and 42 percent of adult women were classified as obese. From 1960 to the 1990s, the prevalence of obesity in children aged six to eleven years increased by 54 percent, and in adolescents aged twelve to seventeen years it increased 39 percent. The prevalence of severe obesity (BMI over 35, over 20 percent above normal weight for height) increased 98 percent in six- to eleven-year-olds and 64 percent in twelve- to seventeen-year-olds.

These statistics are alarming, especially in an affluent society where food is abundant and where most people can easily buy and eat as much food as they wish. It is a serious problem—a major health problem—and I feel that we must consider obesity as we would a disease. A disease starts as a disharmony, an imbalance in the body, the lifestyle, or both. Many Americans haven't been taught how to organize or even think about their food intake in terms of a healthy life. Our plan, later in this book, will help you do that.

OBESITY IS RISKY TO HEALTH

According to a 1998 news release by the National Institutes of Health, five of the ten leading causes of death in the United States have been connected to diet: heart disease, cancer, stroke, hypertension, diabetes, and arteriosclerosis. Over half of the U.S. population is overweight to a degree that has been shown to diminish life expectancy. Obesity is a risk factor in many diseases such as heart disease, hypertension, diabetes, gallbladder disease, gout, osteoarthritis, and sleep apnea. Substantial evidence indicates that nutritional imbalances in the diet contribute to at least 30 percent of cancer deaths in the United States.

The key words in the previous sentence are *nutritional imbalances.* It is not only the *quantity* of food we eat that determines whether we become overweight, but the *quality* and *variety.* Anemia, venous congestion, poor salivation, and autointoxication may also contribute to obesity.

A MEAT-AND-POTATOES MENU IS NOT ENOUGH

The U.S. Department of Agriculture reports that the top-ranked foods in the country are milk products, followed by red meats and wheat products. The following survey results show an interesting food pattern in the United States, one that helps account for the rising obesity and chronic disease statistics. My comments are in parentheses following each item. Of those surveyed:

75 percent eat potatoes at least one in every three days. (Potatoes and meat are a poor age-old combination of which we eat too much.)

61 percent eat red meat every day.

58 percent eat bread every day. (People eat too much bread, squeezing out fruits and vegetables they should have.)

55 percent drink milk every day. (Doctors make a living on people who drink too much milk and eat too much wheat.)

51 percent eat lettuce one in three days. (There is no food value in iceberg lettuce.)

50 percent drink coffee one in three days. (Coffee is not a natural food; there are negative side effects from caffeine.)

50 percent drink soft drinks one in three days. (There are negative side effects from caffeine, saccharine, and sugars we don't need. Also, sugar is high in calories.)

43 percent eat chicken one in three days. (Are there other protein options?)

38 percent drink tea one in three days. (Drink only herb teas.)

36 percent drink orange juice one in three days. (There is not enough variety in juices.)

28 percent eat tomatoes one in three days. (Good.)

17 percent eat bananas one in three days. (Good.)

16 percent eat apples one in three days. (Good.)

15 percent eat frankfurters one in three days. (High in chemical additives.)

10 percent eat cabbage one in three days. (Good.)

10 percent eat hamburgers one in three days. (What else do
  they eat with them? Cola drinks and french fries!)
8 percent drink beer one in three days. (Builds "belly" muscles.)
5 percent drink wine one in three days. (Is it necessary?)
5 percent eat celery one in three days. (Good.)
5 percent eat carrots one in three days. (Good.)

We are squeezing out the amount and variety of fruits and
vegetables that we should eat by concentrating too much on
the foods listed here.

During a recent year, Americans reportedly spent over $30
billion on efforts to control or reduce their weight. Diet foods
alone brought in $20 billion. It's no wonder when we consider
that an estimated fifty billion hamburgers and twenty billion
hot dogs are consumed each year, along with an average of
about six hundred 12-ounce cans of soft drinks per person.
Breakfast cereals, called empty calories by nutritionists, now
include brands with as much sugar content as candy, according
to the Center for Science in the Public Interest. In a pamphlet
titled "Fast Foods and the American Diet," researchers reported
that foods obtained from fast-food restaurants were high in salt
and calories. Americans spent 45 percent of their food dollars
away from home in 1997, up from 39 percent in 1980.

Snacks, fast foods, and junk foods have a minimum of nourishment but are often higher in calories than foods served at
home. Whole, pure, and natural foods increase the probability
that a person will be able to stay near his or her best weight.
Dr. Robert Good of the Memorial Sloan-Kettering Cancer
Center in New York City has said that the person living on an
average 2,800-calorie diet would live longer and stay healthier
if he cut his calories by one-third and his fat intake by one-half.

Dr. George Briggs, professor of Nutrition at the University of California at Berkeley, testified before the U.S. Senate Select Committee on Nutrition and Human Needs that improved nutrition might cut the nation's health bill by one-third.

The USDA's "What We Eat in America" survey shows that fat makes up about 33 percent of the American caloric intake, compared with 15 to 25 percent of the average African or Asian diet. Complex carbohydrates (fresh fruits, vegetables, whole cereal grains, etc.), the dominant source of food energy in the United States in past years, increased by an average of 138 pounds per person per year in 1997 over 1970. Many people get a third of their energy from what I call "foodless foods" that provide calories but almost no vitamins or minerals, like potato chips or high-sugar, cold breakfast cereals. Refined carbohydrates, especially sugar, leach B vitamins from the body; put stress on the pancreas, adrenal glands, and liver; increase putrefaction in the bowel; impede peristaltic motion; and increase blood levels of cholesterol. White sugar, white flour, white rice, and products made from them are the most commonly used refined carbohydrates.

EFFECTS OF BEING OVERWEIGHT

Excess weight poses a variety of physical and mental problems. For one thing, carrying a load of 20 to 40 or more extra pounds all day requires extra energy and food intake. It's like a backpack that can't be taken off when you want to rest, which causes a continual burden on the heart. Because the extra weight stimulates extra eating, it tends to be a self-defeating, fat-sustaining process.

In a 1978 review in the *Canadian Medical Association Journal,* Dr. A. Angel discussed the various changes in the body associated with obesity. Adipose tissue, made up of large round cells that store fat and cholesterol, increases in quantity, supported by collagen tissue and fed by many additionally needed blood vessels. Blood lipids are increased, especially triglycerides. Sugar and alcoholic beverages cause an additional increase in triglycerides. Low-density lipoproteins that carry cholesterol in the bloodstream increase, while high-density lipoproteins, which tend to decrease cholesterol, diminish. Fat breaks down the "good" high-density lipoproteins that normally carry off cholesterol. Cholesterol production by the liver is increased, leading to higher risk of heart disease, while each pound of fat requires miles more of blood vessels, putting extra stress on the heart.

Facts like these, I realize, are not inspirational, and I want to remind you that your goal of becoming the person you want to be is the inspiration that should carry you along. Let these facts work to remind you of how worthwhile and wonderful your goal is, and how much good you will get out of it.

Cardiovascular System

Obesity overworks the heart, increases the chance of heart disease and high blood pressure, and dramatically increases atherosclerosis, the fatty deposit in the linings of artery walls that reduces artery diameter, restricts blood flow, and can lead to heart attack or stroke.

Lymphatic System

The lymphatic system is a network of vessels throughout the body that contains 45 pints of fluid, as compared with 14 pints of blood in the circulatory system. Unlike the blood, the lymph has no "heart" to pump it through its system of vessels. Instead, the lymph is "squeezed" along by muscle contractions during the course of normal physical activity. As people become overweight, the inevitable result is less and less physical activity, which means less and less movement of the lymph. Since the lymph carries nutrients to the cells and waste products from them (among its other activities), the result is congestion and accumulation of catarrh, metabolic wastes, and toxins, which creates a favorable environment for disease. Excess sodium intake increases the amount of water held in the lymph system, a further complication.

Pulmonary System

We find that the greater the bulk of the body, the more oxygen we need, yet the size of the adult lungs is fixed. Because the lungs can't meet the demand for increased oxygen, the cells and tissues of the body work under an oxygen deficit. Abdominal fat presses against the lungs and limits breathing, a further restriction on oxygen intake. All cells and all metabolic processes in the body require oxygen, and we find that oxygen deficiency as a result of being overweight lowers the level of function of every organ, gland, and tissue in the body. Obesity may cause serious complications in cases of asthma.

Gastrointestinal System

The fatty tissue throughout the body of obese persons tends to make the bowel flaccid, leading to prolapse of the transverse colon, balloon conditions, bowel pockets, underactivity, and constipation in many cases. Displacement of the stomach into the chest cavity is more common in overweight individuals.

An overworked, underactive bowel allows more toxic materials to enter the bloodstream, to be deposited in the fatty tissues and inherently weak organs and tissues of the body.

Skeletal System—Joints

Overweight persons experience greater wear and tear on their joints, especially in cases of arthritis or spinal problems, such as slipped or ruptured disks. The discomfort and irritation of painful joints further reduces physical activity in overweight persons, favoring more weight gain and a general increase in associated health problems.

Liver and Gallbladder

Due to lowered physical activity, bowel underactivity, and lymphatic congestion in overweight persons, the liver must work hard to deal with detoxification, reducing its capacity to perform its many other tasks. Because the gallbladder is connected to the liver and receives bile from it, liver malfunction can affect the gallbladder. This may be one reason why more gallbladder disease is found in overweight persons. One study showed that 88 percent of 215 people operated on for gallstones were overweight.

Self-Image Unhappiness

Overweight persons tend to be dissatisfied with their appearance and with the increased physical limitations that come with excess weight. Often there is guilt associated with eating patterns and sensitivity toward comments by others about weight or appearance. They may become depressed or develop low self-esteem.

OVEREATING AND THE MEDIA

Media advertising, in my opinion, contributes greatly to guilt associated with being overweight. Beautiful young men and women with slender, well-proportioned bodies are shown using or promoting products, pretending to have a wonderful time. These ads imply that you have to be young and slender to have a good time.

On the other hand, TV and magazine ads present food after food—candy bars, snack foods, cereals, cakes, cookies, donuts, steaks, waffles, fast foods, and so forth—that look so wonderful they almost appear better than the real thing. So, we are constantly bombarded with ads that encourage us to buy and eat the things that make us fat, while being told we have to look young and slim to enjoy life.

INFLUENCES ON OUR EATING HABITS

In her book *Nutrition and National Policy,* Dr. Beverly Winicoff has pointed out that our eating habits are influenced not only by our upbringing but also by what is available at the supermarket, school cafeteria, restaurants, airports, and places of work. She points out, "We put candy machines in our schools, serve high-fat lunches to our children, and place cigarette machines in our workplaces. The American marketplace provides easy access to sweet soft drinks, high-sugar cereals, candies, cakes, and high-fat beef, and more difficult access to foods likely to improve national nutritional health." Dr. Winicoff states that people seem to believe doctors can cure the various diseases that come from poor eating habits. "There is, in reality, very little that medical science can do to return a patient to normal physiological function," she says. We might add that even hospitals have candy and cigarette machines.

OTHER REASONS WHY PEOPLE ARE OVERWEIGHT

Cultural patterns may induce people to be overweight in several ways. In some countries or regions, excess weight is considered a sign of wealth or high social position. In others, the lifestyle may be slow and easy, allowing more food to be turned into fat. Some cultures keep their women relatively confined to the homes of parents, husbands, or other relatives, which encourages overweight from inactivity and boredom. In a few Middle Eastern countries, overweight women are considered more beautiful. Japanese sumo wrestlers deliberately get as fat as they can and as strong as possible, because both weight and strength are important factors in their sport.

Climate, altitude, terrain, and level of technology influence weight. There are people who gain weight rapidly in wet tropical climates but lose it in a dry or temperate climate. There are people who gain weight at sea level but lose it in the mountains. Hot weather helps some keep slender, while cold weather favors others.

Genetic factors influence weight. I don't exactly like comparing people to horses, but it is useful to realize that some people are built large like draft horses while others are more streamlined like racehorses. There is a "right" weight for each type, but it is not the same, even for the same height. Good curves, by their nature, are looked upon as beautiful, whether the frame is small or large.

When you stop and think about it, there is no such thing as an "average" person. We are all unique. But there is a natural "normal" weight for each of us.

WATER RETENTION AND OBESITY

It has been said that there are some people who can look at a glass of water and gain half a pound on the spot. This is an exaggeration, of course, but there are a considerable number of people who tend to retain water in their tissues, and this is a problem for them. Dr. V. G. Rocine classified such people as hydripheric types or lymph types.

Many women are familiar with a tendency to bloating that comes usually before menstruation each month. In such cases, endocrine hormone shifts are causing water retention. We also find that endocrine imbalance can be an ongoing problem in some persons, holding excess water in the body without regard to the menstrual cycle.

Another cause of water retention is an imbalance in the sodium-potassium ratio in the body. Excessive table salt intake can trigger this imbalance, and the solution is simply to cut back on salt intake and eat more foods that are high in potassium.

Weight-loss gimmicks that promise rapid results often rely on water loss, but they do not burn off enough fat to do any good, so they are useless.

An estimated twenty-five million Americans take diuretic pills to control high blood pressure and many of them have found they can "cheat" a little by using their pills for weight reduction. Diuretics work by causing the excretion of more water, and some have discovered they can lose 6 to 8 pounds in two days. This is extremely dangerous. Potassium, which is very important to the body, is also excreted. Some potassium-depleted patients have had to go on kidney dialysis machines because of kidney damage. Potassium is needed by the muscles, especially the heart muscle, so that loss of this mineral can produce muscle weakness and eventual heart damage. Excess use of diuretics can cause death.

There are safer ways to lose water. Cut back on salt, as previously suggested. KB-11 (Kidney-Bladder) and cleaver tea are herbal diuretics, much safer than diuretic pills. Vitamin B_6 can be used, up to a gram a day, with relative safety. Some who have taken several grams of B_6 per day have experienced problems with the nerves in their wrists. It is possible to overdose with some vitamins, so it is best to investigate what the maximum safe level is.

FAD DIETS ARE NOT THE ANSWER

Every year, millions of Americans go through the ritual of starving their bodies down to some desired weight, only to gain it all back again in the next few months. They take special diet pills, powdered mixes, eat certain fruits, and stay away from fattening foods—for a while. Then they fall back into their old living habits again. Newspaper columnist Ralph Moyed estimated that he has lost 485 pounds since 1977 trying various diets and visits to "fat farms," as he calls them, and has gained nearly all of it back. Many people are familiar with the yo-yo process of gaining and losing weight, over and over.

In 1998, approximately 181 million Americans were on diets. Dean Ornish, M.D., reports that 66 percent of dieters regain their former weight within a year, while 97 percent gain it back within five years. Most of us have heard about the grapefruit diet. Then came the steak and tomato diet, the drinking man's diet, the macrobiotic diet, and now the cabbage soup diet. In the 1970s, seventeen people died from trying to live solely on a popular liquid diet drink. There are at least twenty-nine current diet powders designed to be mixed with liquids on the market as meal replacements. An estimated nine million Americans have tried diet powders.

The danger of these diet powders is that many provide only 330 to 500 calories a day, which is basically a starvation or fasting diet. Muscle wasting, water loss, nutritional imbalance, endocrine system imbalance, fatigue, and other serious health problems can occur as a result of following such a diet. No diet under 1,000 calories per day for women or 1,500 calories per day for men should be attempted without a doctor's supervision or advice.

We find that the average person is simply not well enough informed about food, nutrition, and the workings of the body to safely conduct a fast or an extreme low-calorie program of weight loss. Losing weight too rapidly may damage the organs and glands and nearly always creates a rebound effect. Over 95 percent of those who use rapid weight-loss diets to reduce their weight gain it back within a year, according to Dr. George Blackburn of Harvard Medical School.

If fad diets, diet powders, and diet pills were the solution to the problem of obesity, it would have been solved long ago. We need to realize, however, that it is not the diet program that loses or gains weight, it is the person. It is necessary to pay attention to and take care of the person at the other end of the weight problem to achieve lasting, permanent results.

The ritual of periodic, repeated dieting to take care of periodic, repeated weight gain is only a symptom of a more basic underlying problem. I don't believe the problem is the same for everyone. We are all unique individuals, different in the ways we think and feel, different in the ways our bodies respond to foods, different in the ways we handle the stresses and experiences of life. We don't have the same size or strength in the functional ability of our organs. There is a solution to undesirable weight gain, and it can only be found by seeking a right way of living and sticking to it.

NATURE SHOWS THE WAY

For over sixty years, I have worked with patients, using natural methods to bring people back to health. Many of those years were spent in sanitarium settings in which I lived and worked with my patients day after day, week after week, trying to help each one find a permanent solution to their ailments or conditions. I discovered that nature cures, but sometimes she needs help.

Chronic disease builds up in the body in most cases from faulty eating and living habits over a period of years. In this sense, obesity can many times be classified as a chronic disease. Fat develops slowly, just like many chronic diseases, when the metabolism has been thrown off balance. The best way to take care of it is to look to nature for the answer, just as I have done in taking care of other health problems.

The problem with modern civilization and a high standard of living is that man looks away from the great encyclopedia of nature and bases his lifestyle on what contemporary technology has to offer. Too many people take on a self-indulgent philosophy, get into the fast lane of life, and proceed to eat, drink, work, smoke, and worry themselves into disease. The way back to a permanent state of health lies in reversing the process by which the disease was acquired, not in some temporary treatment of symptoms. Treating symptoms does not remove the cause.

THE REVERSAL PROCESS

The first step on the reversal path is to stop doing those things that contribute to the problem or disease. The second step involves cleansing the body of debris and toxic waste that are contributing to the problem. Cleansing may be helped by diet, properly supervised fasting, bowel management techniques, exercise or hard physical work, selected herbs and other supplements, and reducing the stress of life problems. When the body tissue has been adequately cleansed, the next step is to go to a food regimen based on whole, pure, and natural foods. Tissue can only be rejuvenated or rebuilt with nutrients from foods. My Thirty-Day Diet Plan will help cleanse the body as well as reduce the weight. Reducing the amount of fatty tissue on the body is essentially a reversal process, with many side benefits.

There were no can openers in the Garden of Eden. Adam and Eve had no frying pan, and they were not tempted by hundreds of TV ads to eat sugary or salty or fat-fried foods devoid of most nutritional value. They did not plug up their bowels with processed fiberless foods, nor did they go out to fast-food restaurants twice a week. Their foods were natural, pure, and whole, and they had no diseases and no excess fat. Fad diets would not exist if we had not departed so far from the food principles of the Garden of Eden.

Most diets aim at getting rid of the symptom—fat. My diet plan is different. My approach is to help you understand why you are overweight, then assist you in discovering a better, more natural, and appropriate food regimen and lifestyle, a way of life that will bring you sufficient peace and satisfaction that you can leave diets behind and simply live a healthy way of life.

When we find the higher path in life, willpower increases to a level where we take control over what we eat, think, feel, and do with ourselves. As our lives improve, so does our willpower. We need willpower. We need to know that we are doing the right thing. Psychologists say that the strength of our willpower is related to general muscle tone. My program is designed for adults who are willing to use their willpower to do the right thing in their lives.

Reaching a weight that is right for you and staying there depends upon your willingness to recognize and leave behind those aspects of your lifestyle that cause overweight. The reward is great—good health is a door through which we must walk to find the best things in life.

I believe there is a natural weight for everybody. It may not be exactly what the statistical charts say we should weigh, but it is the proper weight where each individual is disease free and feels at his or her best.

CHAPTER 2

WHY YOU GAIN WEIGHT

There are many reasons why people put on extra "padding," some psychological and some physical. However, we too often find that experts attempt to separate the mental realm from the physical realm, leaving us with two disconnected sets of explanations for problems such as obesity, and this can be misleading. Everything that happens to the body or inside the body affects the mind; every thought, emotion, perception, attitude, or belief affects the body.

Disease can cause obesity, and obesity can cause disease. Studies have shown the mortality rate from diabetes in men over age forty-five increases ten times in those who are 26 percent overweight as compared to normal-weight men. Obesity has been associated with diabetes as both a possible cause and an effect, even though the direct cause is pancreas malfunction. When the blood sugar is abnormal, food cravings are abnormal, and the reverse is also true. Scientists don't know the ultimate cause of diabetes.

Anemia, endocrine problems, venous congestion, lymphatic congestion, and inadequate salivation may all contribute to obesity. Children overfed as infants may develop more fat cells than others, which can cause lifelong problems with weight control.

Overeating has many psychological factors involving self-image, the emotions, boredom, stress response, and personality. The psychological and physical aspects of obesity do not exist separately or independently from one another, so we will look at them together.

WHAT DETERMINES HOW WE FEEL ABOUT OUR WEIGHT?

According to Susan C. Wooley, former codirector of the Eating Disorders Clinic at the University of Cincinnati Medical Center, the current obsession with thinness is producing serious problems in today's women. She feels that today's generation of young women is the first to grow up watching their mothers, *the first generation of weight watchers, despairing over their thighs.* In one survey, only 13 percent of the young women participating believed their mothers liked their own bodies. Unhappy with themselves, the majority of the mothers tended to be critical of their daughters.

I have treated five cases of anorexia in the past few years, and, believe me, many women are having a very difficult time putting food and lifestyle patterns into a right perspective. I teach my patients that proper eating is to be appreciated as a means of letting the best in life flow through us.

In some countries of the Middle East today, most notably Turkey, men consider plump women more attractive. Some years ago, the film *Mondo Cane* featured an African tribal monarch with a considerable number of wives, all hugely obese. Obese wives were not only considered beautiful in that African culture but were status symbols as well. It took a fair amount of wealth to keep a wife that well fed.

The slender feminine ideal today in the United States is just the opposite. It is almost impossible to achieve in the context of the average home life or job. Models and actresses seen in films, in magazines, and on TV are paid extremely high wages compared to the average woman, and it is as much a part of their job to be thin as it is to act or to model. They say a woman at her normal ideal weight appears fat on TV. Almost any woman in this country could stay thin if she were paid a thousand dollars a week or so for her trouble. Yet, only two generations ago, some men preferred women who were "pleasingly plump." This is something to stop and think about.

We find that the basic problems of those who have anorexia nervosa and bulimia are centered around a fixation on slenderness, a fear of being fat, and an addiction to dieting. Dr. John Kilbourne, a university lecturer and authority on advertising, states, "Ads are a very powerful educational force. It's difficult not to be influenced by the constant bombardment." He notes that ads tend to make women feel guilty about being overweight. In fact, diet and weight-loss products are marketed by making women feel insecure about their bodies, since they see only thin women in all the ads. Basically, this is a form of psychological manipulation, and we should not be deceived by it.

The same media pressure is exerted toward men, but not to the same degree of success, perhaps because men are not as sensitive to the emotional undercurrents used in ads as women are.

Still, there is definitely something very wrong with a society in which women and men are influenced to feel guilty and unhappy about their bodies. There is something very wrong when 20 percent of all teenage girls have used vomiting to control their weight, as reported by Susan Wooley of the University of Cincinnati. When we find millions of women using fast weight-loss programs to the point of triggering natural body defenses and later bringing out a compulsive urge to gorge on food, we need to realize that we are not doing the right thing.

A young woman in her twenties weighing 86 pounds came to my office at the Ranch with anorexia. For seven years, her eating was influenced mostly by mental attitude—avoiding certain foods, choosing others, trying various diets, until her system was so imbalanced that she became seriously underweight. We put her on a harmony way of living at the Ranch, and in a few months, her weight was up to 116 pounds. She followed our basic Health and Harmony Food Regimen, substituting vegetarian proteins for the fish, poultry, lamb, and occasional lean beef allowed. When I asked her what had contributed most to overcoming her condition, she said, "You've done more toward changing my attitude toward food than anything else." I feel that professional counseling is a must for overcoming any anorexia or bulimia problem.

Wrong eating habits can have a powerful effect on the nervous system, the glandular system, or both, and the mind can become seriously affected. Starvation diets ultimately damage the nerves and force the glandular system and body to adjust to a lower metabolic rate. Fatigue and depression set in all too easily, along with irritability and sudden mood shifts. Psychological problems become intermingled with physical problems, and the solution to these problems will never be found until we discover that nature has something very important to teach us. We need to get away from extremes and look to nature to find out a right way to live.

When we eat right, get adequate rest, fresh air, sunshine, and so forth, our bodies will adjust to a weight matched to a natural state of high-level well-being. You can feel wonderful. You can enjoy your body and experience the best health you've ever had. But you must be willing to work for it!

INHERITANCE AND INHERENT WEAKNESSES

Some people gain weight easier than others, and I believe much of this could be inherited. All doctors recognize that some people are born with weak lungs, weak kidneys, liver defects, and so on. I call organs and tissues that do not function normally "inherent weaknesses," and all of us have at least a few of them. Some have many.

When we are born, we are one-third our father, one-third our mother, and one-third ourselves. We can have a normal body even though we may have inherent weaknesses brought down from the father, mother, or farther back on the family tree. We may have inherited a tendency to gain weight, or we may become overweight from poor food habits traditionally used in the family. Studies have shown that obese children are three times as likely to become obese adults. However, we have dominion over our bodies, and we can compensate for most inherent weaknesses.

An extreme genetic tendency to gain weight, in my opinion, could take five to eight generations to overcome by following right living and eating methods in each generation.

We need to recognize that there are consequences when we have inherent weaknesses. The person with a pancreas weakness can't tolerate sugar the way other people can. The person with an underactive bowel can't take care of white flour products or fiberless foods the way other people can. In other words, we have to take special care of our inherent weaknesses to keep the weaker organs and tissues from breaking down and becoming vulnerable to disease or influencing our weight.

A tendency to gain weight easily may be due to a variety of inherited conditions. Because there are so many glands, nerves, and organs involved in appetite, digestion, assimilation, and use of nutrients, inherent weakness in one or more of them can make fatty tissue production a potential problem. In most cases, as I have mentioned, we can compensate for inherent weaknesses by proper eating, proper exercise, and a proper mental attitude.

Among the glands and organs that are involved with fat metabolism are the hypothalamus, pituitary gland, thyroid gland, pancreas, adrenals, sex glands, liver, gallbladder, and small intestine. If inherent weaknesses are found in any of these glands and organs, we may have problems with weight control.

Some persons metabolize their foods faster. Some digest foods more efficiently, perhaps because of an abundance of digestive juices. Some have better mental attitudes toward food, health, and themselves.

Genetic defects, as found in some glands causing a lack of certain enzymes, can also affect fat metabolism.

HOW THE GLANDS AFFECT WEIGHT GAIN

One of the undesirable side effects of low-calorie fad diets under 1,000 calories a day is the "starvation" response by the brain. When weight is lost too rapidly, the thyroid gland slows down to adjust the metabolism to the lower food intake, so fewer fat calories are burned. Meanwhile, the appetite center in the hypothalamus turns on the "hunger switch." As normal eating habits are later restored, a higher percentage of the food is turned to fat because the body energy requirements have been lowered, and the "hunger switch" in the brain stays on until all the old lost weight has been "found" again. These diets are self-defeating because of the way our brains work.

The pituitary is the master gland of the endocrine gland system, and doctors have found that tumors of the pituitary and other types of pituitary malfunction can contribute to obesity. The pituitary is connected to the hypothalamus of the brain (where the appetite center is) by nerves and blood vessels. Neurohormones secreted by the hypothalamus influence the secretions of the pituitary, which, in turn, affect the various other glands. Keep in mind that the appetite center is associated with blood levels of various nutrients, and I believe this also has an influence on the pituitary.

Why are these things important? Because imbalance of the sex hormone estrogen can trigger obesity, and the adrenal hormone aldosterone controls water retention in the body. The amount of salt we use in foods, among other factors, affects the aldosterone level in the body. Fasting diets can disrupt the glandular system by dramatically altering nutrient levels and balances in the body, leading to abnormal weight gain later. The short-term success in weight loss leads to long-term failure. We must know about these things to avoid the pitfalls that catch so many dieters.

Dr. Weston Price, author of the classic *Nutrition and Physical Degeneration,* believed that a diet high in refined carbohydrates, particularly white sugar, threw the endocrine system out of balance. An imbalanced endocrine system can open the door to many disorders, but one of the most common is obesity.

A malfunctioning pituitary gland, an underactive thyroid, adrenals that cannot control the sodium-potassium balance in the blood, and imbalanced estrogen production can all contribute to obesity. Emotional upset, sexual frustration, depression, and even boredom may lead to unwanted weight gain.

The glands need lecithin, protein, and cholesterol to function properly. Cholesterol, seldom deficient in the body, needs to be balanced by lecithin. Those with high blood cholesterol, generally speaking, would do better to take more lecithin than to cut back on cholesterol in foods, although I do not approve of fatty meats or fat-fried foods for other reasons than cholesterol content. We find that the thyroid needs adequate iodine to function properly, and we can get iodine from halibut, sea bass, tuna, salmon, red snapper, rock cod, fish roe, kelp products, dulse, onions, and various fruits and vegetables grown near the sea coast.

MENOPAUSAL WEIGHT GAIN

Weight gain after menopause is often a very frustrating experience for a woman because the changes in body chemistry are so complex it is difficult to know what to do. I believe the best way to approach change-of-life weight problems is to make sure the body has all the minerals needed to come to its new equilibrium as gracefully as possible.

Menopause weight gain is usually due to endocrine system adjustments as discussed in the previous section. Sometimes the herbs black cohosh and licorice are very helpful to women going through the change of life, and men will find that ginseng and fo ti tieng will help balance the glands.

Adequate exercise is needed to keep the body toned, the blood and lymph circulating, and the bowel functioning properly. Exercise is even more vital in the later years than for the young, but strenuous exercise should be avoided by those unaccustomed to it.

THE MENTAL SIDE OF THE WEIGHT PROBLEM

It is fascinating to consider that the appetite center is in the hypothalamus, which has been called the psychosomatic center of the brain. Nerves from every tissue and organ in the body converge on this brain center, as well as nerves from the emotional and thinking areas of the brain. The hypothalamus is where thoughts and emotions affect the blood chemistry and the automatic functions of the body, down to the cell level, and, conversely, where the blood chemistry and metabolic functions affect the thoughts and emotions. The way we think and feel can help us become fat or thin.

I had a patient once who failed to lose weight despite being on an excellent reducing regimen I had given him. When I questioned him about it, he admitted he was eating a whole broiled chicken every night because he had a deep-seated fear of not getting his fair share of food. He overate because of a fear of not getting enough.

The housekeeper of the famous violinist Fritz Kreisler could tell by the kind of music he was practicing what kind of meals to serve him. If he was playing difficult classical music, he was exacting in his meals. But if he was playing waltzes or other light music, he wasn't so strict in what he wanted to eat. In his case, music affected his mood, mood affected his mind, and his mind was then affected in its food choices.

There are people who feel they have to "keep up with the Joneses" in the expense, quantity, and refinement of the foods they eat. If you serve food you think your guests will like, you have to eat it, too. Most of us have had the experience of going out with people, then ordering what they order (or ordering what we think will impress them), whether it is good for us or not. Similarly, we have all been guests at the homes of others where we had to eat what they served. You can see how the mind affects how we handle ourselves in such cases. We can usually eat more of the vegetables and leave the refined starches alone. We have to be selective to eat properly, regardless of circumstances. Figure 2.1 indicates some reasons why Americans say they fail to maintain their desired weight.

There are many times, I think, that instead of eating we should get busy at some job or hobby or *take a walk*—anything to take the place of the craving for food. Many times these cravings are abnormal and don't represent a real need for food. Some people are like Pavlov's dog—whenever the bell rings, they are ready to eat. Others are stuck in schedules. They always have breakfast at 7 A.M., lunch at noon, and supper at 6 P.M. Their minds are trained to think "food" at certain times whether the stomach is hungry or not. I feel it is not a good idea to eat unless we are hungry.

We find that many people allow food to draw them around like a bull with a ring in its nose. When it is time to eat, we eat, not because we have to but because it is a habit. Eating or drinking should not be a hobby, avocation, or something we always think of when we have time or money on our hands. Many people can't get their minds off food, which can cause them a lot of trouble.

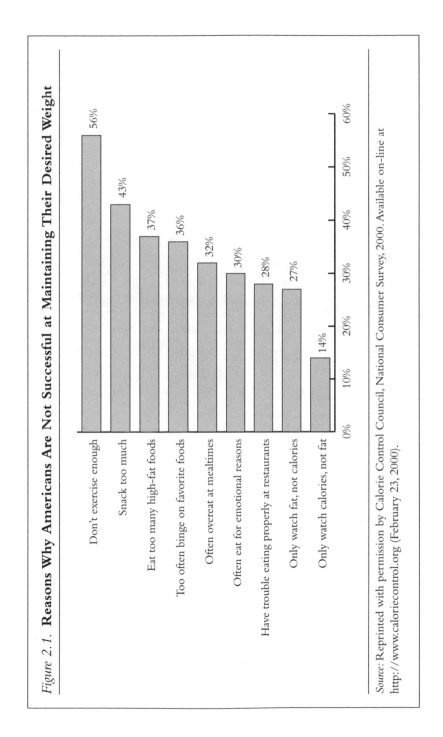

Figure 2.1. **Reasons Why Americans Are Not Successful at Maintaining Their Desired Weight**

Source: Reprinted with permission by Calorie Control Council, National Consumer Survey, 2000. Available on-line at http://www.caloriecontrol.org (February 23, 2000).

Some people don't eat, they "breathe" their food in. They take in everything they can. They work on their plates like they are vacuuming a rug. Once we had a group at the Ranch who complained that they didn't get enough to eat when we served the food on plates, so I put the food out in buffet style and let them help themselves. One man filled his plate four times at one meal, and I told him, "You are going to kill yourself eating all that food." He said, "I'm paying for it, so I'm going to get all I can." This is a bad attitude, and sometimes our attitude is what kills us. We find out that we are capable of eating enough to fill a much larger dress or suit than we should fill, and this is where we need to apply common sense and discipline.

Some people overeat when they are bored, depressed, unhappy, or feel unloved. Others lose their appetites when they fall in love, lose their jobs, have an argument with their spouses, or suffer an emotional shock of any kind.

One survey claimed that 87 percent of the mothers of teenage girls probably do not like their bodies. What does a thought like that do to the appetite center? When we look at the extreme effects of emotion and thought in anorexia and bulimia cases, it is overwhelmingly evident that what goes on in our minds has much to do with how we eat, what we eat, how much and how often we eat, and how our bodies process what goes into them.

Cigarettes, amphetamines, and diet pills all suppress the appetite center by drugging it, but as soon as the drug is taken away, more weight is put on than before. Suppression never really works and is almost always counterproductive in the long run. Unnatural forms of weight loss probably all have undesirable side effects and long-term effects.

PERCEPTION AND OVEREATING

We know the brain monitors glucose levels in the blood and is capable of triggering hunger in the appetite center when glucose falls too low. But we can also become stimulated to hunger, even when the body has adequate nutrients circulating, by the sight or smell of food. So we know the visual and smell centers of the brain are connected to the appetite center.

Unfortunately, foods that are bad for us can be very appealing, and a bad diet can cause obesity.

BRAIN CONTROL OF WEIGHT AND APPETITE

In recent years, some researchers have come to believe that some part of the brain "decides" on how much fat our bodies need, and that we eat until we have it. I believe this is nonsense, because if it were true, many people in other countries besides ours who have access to plenty of food would be "overweight," and we find that obesity is more of a problem in the United States than in most other places.

What I believe is that the body may get used to the amount of fat it contains, and some center in the brain considers this fat "normal" after a period of months or years. After all, fat is not dead matter. It has blood vessels and nerves running through it. It affects the center of balance, the blood chemistry, the amount of work the heart does, and many other functions.

If the brain considers a certain amount of fat natural to the body, it will be alarmed at rapid weight loss, assuming it indicates potential imbalance of body chemistry and function. This is why the metabolism drops, to conserve energy and to keep functions going at a lower level of energy use and food intake.

The brain's appetite center is very patient and stores up a long-term hunger, which is geared for new weight gain once the diet is ended. *All permanent weight-loss programs must take this effect into account to be successful.* There is at least one way to overcome this problem, which we will take up later.

Scientists once thought that overweight people were psychologically different from people who were not overweight. More recent research indicates that psychological differences come after the weight gain and because of it, not before.

THE DIGESTIVE PROCESS AND OBESITY

Most overweight problems boil down to overeating, but they also occur because of dietary deficiencies—lack of fiber or water, for example. When we eat more of the right foods, we eat less of the wrong foods. When we neglect to eat the right foods, we develop chemical deficiencies in the body. Chemical deficiencies can lead to obesity. It's as simple as that. Even knowing how the digestive process works can help us learn to keep the food intake under control.

When we eat, digestion begins in the mouth as salivary enzymes begin changing starches into sugars. In the stomach, the food is churned up, broken down into fine particles, and mixed with hydrochloric acid and enzymes. Protein is broken down into molecules called polypeptides. The liquefied stomach contents are squirted into the beginning of the small intestine. Pancreatic enzymes plus bile from the liver are secreted into the small intestine. The pancreas completes the digestion of starches and assists in the breakdown of proteins and fats. Fats are emulsified by the bile and made ready for absorption. Tiny, fingerlike projections along the small intestine called *villi* then begin picking up the digested, broken-down microscopic food particles and absorbing them into the bloodstream.

All food-carrying blood vessels from the small intestine empty into a single large blood vessel, which goes to the liver. The liver, one of the largest and most important organs in the body, processes proteins, fats, and starches. Components of proteins called amino acids are sent out for cell building and repair, glucose is sent to cells for energy, and fats are sent out bearing the fat-soluble vitamins, such as A and E. The liver stores extra glucose as glycogen, but when its storage requirements are met, the excess glucose is converted into fatty acids. Excess proteins may be broken down into waste acids, such as urea, and excreted through the kidneys, but they may also be converted to blood sugars or fat. A common misconception is that a high-protein, low-carbohydrate, low-fat diet is an effective reducing diet. Not necessarily. You may have a digestive problem. Your doctor may recommend digestion aids and Pancreatin with meals. As I said before, any food can add extra weight under certain circumstances. We need to think in terms of a balanced food regimen.

OBESITY AND THE BOWEL

The importance of bowel regularity and colon hygiene had been all but forgotten by the great majority of doctors until very recently. A sluggish colon, constipation, and bowel irregularity have two consequences that favor obesity in a certain type of people. The longer waste material remains in the bowel, the more fats and cholesterol are absorbed into the bloodstream. The same is true of toxic waste products. The latter circulate in the bloodstream, and some appear to get past the liver, the great detoxifier of the body, to deposit in inherently weak glands and organs. Toxic settlements lower the metabolism of tissue where they settle, which in some cases allows greater buildup of fat.

SUMMARY

The following list summarizes the causes currently known as the roots of obesity and unwanted weight gain.

1. Overeating

When we eat more calories than we use up in daily activities, we gain weight—mostly fat.

2. Genetic Inheritance

Our inherent weaknesses can predispose us to obesity. We may lack enzymes needed to break down fat and expel it.

3. Endocrine Imbalance

Imbalance in the endocrine glandular system can cause obesity, particularly the pituitary, thyroid, pancreas, adrenals, and sex glands.

4. Poor Diet

A poor diet can cause obesity directly or through endocrine imbalance.

5. Menopause

This is basically a glandular system adjustment.

6. Rapid Weight-Loss Diets

These usually encourage even more rapid weight gain afterward.

7. Psychological Problems

Many people tend to snack and overeat when they are bored, depressed, unhappy, and feel unloved. Feelings of insecurity may contribute to overeating.

8. Brain Centers

Brain centers tend to protect the status quo, even when the status quo is unwanted fat. The basic problem is still overeating.

9. Digestive Problems

Liver or pancreas malfunctions may have an effect on weight gain, but may be caused by poor eating habits in the first place. A toxic bowel or a constipated bowel encourages reabsorption of cholesterol from bile and toxic deposits in tissues, which lowers metabolism and encourages weight gain.

10. Deficiencies

What we *don't eat* as well as what we *do eat* can cause nutrient deficiencies in the body that encourage weight gain. Lack of exercise contributes to extra pounds.

11. Family Environment

If one or both parents are significantly overweight, the probability that the children will become overweight is markedly increased.

CHAPTER 3

HOW MUCH SHOULD YOU WEIGH?

W hen the Creator designed the human body, I don't believe He intended to have it come out assembly-line style, with all women destined to weigh 123 pounds and all men 165 pounds. There are individual differences that give us a certain amount of leeway in these matters, and it is best to make our peace with the fact that we are not all going to look like movie stars or models.

We need to learn to be the best we can be, then accept what we are and be glad about it. In the previous chapter, we saw how most standards of beauty—whether fat, medium, or thin—are determined culturally. There is no inherent reason why we should let other people decide how much we should weigh or how we should look. I believe nature knows best, and if we look to her for our answers, we will not be disappointed. If we try to be something we are not, we are asking for trouble.

No one can say with absolute assurance what you should weigh. But one can get close. Scientific research, population studies, statistics, and insurance company studies have contributed greatly to our understanding of how much a person of a certain height and build should weigh to have the healthiest possible life. So, we know closely, if not exactly, how much you should weigh.

THE NOTION OF "IDEAL WEIGHT"

I believe there is an ideal weight for everyone, a weight naturally suited to us by virtue of our height, skeletal framework, metabolism, and inheritance. The problem is, *no formula discovered by science can calculate this.*

Some researchers say that if you are somewhat above or below your "ideal" weight and you feel well and fit, don't worry about it. We can't force everyone into the same mold. I believe it could be possible that weight should vary, at least slightly, with occupation. That is, if the same person had a job doing active physical labor for three years, then transferred to a desk job, I would expect some readjustment of the body in terms of metabolism, enzyme activity, nutrient processing, and weight gain.

When I traveled around the world searching for the secrets of longevity by talking to the oldest men and women in each country, many of them over 120 years old, I found that most weighed the same as they had from age twenty to thirty. These people were in excellent health. Other researchers say a slow, steady weight gain of a pound per year is to be expected as we grow older. I suspect this is mainly true of those who elect to follow a sedentary lifestyle, but hormonal changes and lowering of basal metabolism are inevitable with aging, and both lead to weight gain.

Still another research project indicates that if people stayed slightly under their ideal weights, they might live up to 30 percent longer. The study was done with laboratory rats who were consistently underfed, compared to a control group of rats who were allowed to eat all they wanted. When I visited the Hunza Valley some years ago, many of the old men and women, still healthy although well over 100 years old, were as slim as they had been in their twenties. They seemed to eat less at meals than the average person in the United States.

Not all ideas of what makes a healthy or beautiful body center around ideal weight. Adolf Just, author of *Return to Nature: Paradise Regained,* believed that body symmetry was more important. He measured what he called "Grecian curves" and came up with a unique standard for what constitutes a healthy body, based on looks instead of weight. I believe he used the term *Grecian curves* because the ancient Greek concept of feminine beauty embraced fuller-bodied women than today's standards in Western nations.

Let's realize that the ultimate goal must be a healthy body, a body free of disease with plenty of vitality and high-level well-being. If you try to sustain a weight that is too slim for your constitution, you will not feel your best physically or mentally.

There are different charts for ideal weight, and the one we use is among the best.

Because of body chemistry and hormonal differences, women carry more adipose tissue on their bodies than do men, which accounts for their soft, graceful curvature.

Children, from infancy through the teens, may go through changes in body fat related to changing metabolism and body chemistry, but I want to make clear that obesity in children is just as hard on them, with almost the same risks and dangers, as it is on adults. The reasons children become overweight are about the same as for adults. In overeating, the only difference is that the parent, not the child, bears responsibility.

THE RIGHT WAY TO COUNT CALORIES

Almost everyone has some idea of what calories are from watching television advertisements of diet soft drinks. Too many calories make us fat, and fewer calories will keep us slimmer. This is approximately true, but it is certainly not sufficient to help us know what a healthy food regimen is. We need to understand that *all* foods have calories, but only whole, pure, natural foods build health.

A *calorie,* as defined in nutritional studies, *is the amount of heat energy required to raise the temperature of a kilogram of water 1 degree Celsius.* The calories in most common foods have been determined by laboratory tests, and the calories of work energy it takes to perform different kinds of activities and jobs have also been measured. It is not difficult to compute how many calories we need per day to get through the various things we do and add the calories it takes to run the body's metabolism. That determines how many calories we need in our food intake each day. (See Table 3.1.)

If we take in more calories than we use, the excess turns into fat. When we realize that it takes 3,500 calories to make a pound of fat, we can see how one soft drink a day (which comes to 55,000 calories a year!) can cause us to put on nearly 16 pounds of weight annually. This is why we have to watch what we eat, especially when we are past the active "calorie-burning years"—from the teens to the late thirties.

Table 3.1. **Daily Dietary Calories Needed**

	Females				Males		
Age	Ideal Weight	Height (in.)	Calories	Age	Ideal Weight	Height (in.)	Calories
10–12	77	56	2,250	10–12	77	55	2,500
12–14	97	61	2,300	12–14	95	59	2,700
14–16	114	62	2,400	14–18	130	67	3,000
16–18	119	63	2,300	18–22	147	69	2,800
18–22	128	64	2,000	22–35	154	69	2,800
22–35	128	64	2,000	35–55	154	68	2,600
35–55	128	63	1,850	55–75+	154	67	2,400
55–75+	128	62	1,700				

In my travels around the world, I have met many old men and a few old women who were perfectly healthy and over a hundred years old. Not one of them used a high-calorie diet. Not one of them overate or used junk foods.

THE QUALITY OF CALORIES COUNTS MOST

It isn't only the number of calories that counts but the quality of foods we get them from. The National Academy of Sciences has recommended that our daily intake of food calories average 10 to 15 percent protein, less than 30 percent fat, and 55 to 60 percent carbohydrates. This is less protein and fat and more carbohydrates than the average American adult consumes, but it is basically a healthier diet. We also need a certain amount of water, vitamins, and minerals each day.

My Health and Harmony Food Regimen, described in chapter 6, will make clear what I consider quality foods. I just want to say that I don't believe in junk foods, fried foods, refined carbohydrates (such as white sugar and white flour), or packaged foods, which are usually dead foods preserved by chemicals. None of these foods is natural to our bodies, and I believe they are often fattening and always harmful to our health, no matter how many or few calories they have. Abnormal foods build abnormal bodies.

People have come to consider anything they put into their mouths as food, but that is not true. When we stop and think about it, only those substances that promote life and health in us qualify as foods. Real food is essential for the growth, life, repair, and replacement of cells and tissues, and it gives us the energy we need to function in our daily lives. Most kinds of food are composed of seven basic elements—water, protein, carbohydrates, fats, fiber, minerals, and vitamins.

Processed "foods" often lack sufficient vitamins and minerals to properly process and use the protein, carbohydrates, and fat they contain. That's why I call them "foodless foods," and others refer to them as "empty calories."

The best foods for us are foods that are whole, natural, pure, and fresh. I believe in plenty of fresh fruits and vegetables eaten mostly raw. I believe in using fresh meat whenever possible, preferably fish (the kind with white meat, fins, and scales), chicken, turkey, lamb, and, occasionally, lean beef. I do not believe in eating fatty meats, pork, or manufactured meat products such as hot dogs. Meat should be broiled, roasted, or baked, and vegetables should be cooked in waterless stainless steel cookware or steamed to preserve the enzymes, vitamins, and minerals as much as possible. Potatoes, yams, and sweet potatoes may be baked in their skins (eat them sparingly). Potatoes should be eaten with skins to provide minerals, vitamins, and fiber.

THE BASICS OF WEIGHT LOSS

If it takes 3,500 calories of food to build a pound of fat, it will take 3,500 calories of energy to burn up that same pound. The basic strategy in weight loss is to use up more calories than you eat each day, which means you must exercise more, eat less, or do both. Eating less has faster results, and I would add that if we reduce wisely and eat quality food (although less of it), we will stay healthy and well during and after the diet.

Because it takes more calories simply to maintain an overweight body than one at the ideal weight, we can expect to encounter an energy lag at some point as we shift from a higher to a lower weight. The less junk food, coffee, alcohol, and other valueless food and drink you take in, the more available energy you will have, but any energy drop you experience is only temporary.

As explained in chapter 2, the brain doesn't know you are dieting but sees the lower food intake as starvation, which brings an inherent survival mechanism into play. The thyroid slows down energy use throughout the body, and metabolism slows down to balance with the lower food use. This is what brings about the energy lag. At the same time, the brain stores in its memory the fact that the body is losing weight, which will be regained later. This weight "deficit" is then activated when the person goes off the diet. All this is done below the level of consciousness with all fast weight-loss diets.

Another thing going on is that all the enzymes in the body, which were busy building and maintaining fat, are still there, but many of them are now "unemployed," so to speak. These "unemployed" enzymes are thought to play a role in both the relentless hunger response after the diet and the rebound weight-gain effect.

Keep in mind, we are talking about rapid weight loss, which I do not endorse or approve of unless done under a doctor's supervision. Rapid weight loss can cause all sorts of problems for the body and mind, and such diets are usually counterproductive. Research shows that 95 percent of those who lose weight on crash diets gain it back within a year.

The correct way to lose weight is to take it off slowly enough that the brain, nerves, and endocrine glands can adjust to the new weight without triggering the starvation response and bringing in the rebound weight-gain effect. Impatience is our worst enemy in dieting. We want to see results at the bathroom scale—fast. It can be done fast, as we know from experience. But it is time to face the facts and recognize that rapid weight loss with low-caloric diets simply doesn't work. The fat comes back.

MORE THAN WILLPOWER IS NEEDED

We find that we can't override the innate wisdom and survival instinct of the body with sheer willpower alone because the brain mechanisms involved have nothing to do with willpower.

Some years ago, a clever research scientist devised a diet experiment with a group of volunteers to see if automatic brain-regulating mechanisms could be fooled. The volunteers were given access to automatic push-button dispensers of a liquid diet drink and were told they could drink as much as they wanted, just as long as they wrote down the amount in a record book. The liquid was tasty, nutritionally balanced, and fortified with vitamins and minerals. It had a carefully measured number of calories per glass.

After several days, when the researcher knew the amount of the liquid each person drank per day (and the number of calories), he cut the number of calories in half without telling the people. That is, he diluted the drink in such a way that the taste, consistency, and appearance remained the same. Only the calories were changed, which the subjects had no way of knowing.

The first day of the change, most people drank their usual amount. The second day, all increased their intake. Within several days, all subjects had doubled their liquid diet consumption, giving them the same number of calories they had before.

The brain is not fooled by the sight, smell, and taste of food into taking too few calories.

Related experiments were done with rats at the Massachusetts Institute of Technology, and researchers found that carbohydrate intake increased the amount of the neurotransmitter serotonin, which decreased the hunger signal from the brain when the rats had eaten enough. The serotonin apparently builds up in the brain and shuts off the "switch" in the appetite center when a sufficient number of carbohydrate calories have been taken in. Researchers varied the taste of the rats' food, but they still ate the same daily total amount of carbohydrates. They varied the percentage of carbohydrates and the rats still ate the same amount. Regulatory control over carbohydrate intake had to be in the brain, since taste, smell, sight, and varied percentages of carbohydrates in the feed showed no influence over the rats' total carbohydrate consumption.

Researchers then investigated dieters using high-protein, low-carbohydrate reducing diets. After dieters came off their diets, researchers found that it took twice as much carbohydrate as before the diet to build up the same serotonin level. In other words, the high-protein, low-carbohydrate diet had somehow messed up the carbohydrate-regulating system in the body, and those who were trying to eat normal meals again were not feeling satisfied until they had eaten twice as much starchy foods and sugary foods per day as they had before they started dieting. This is the rebound effect. This is why many people regain all of or more than the weight lost while dieting.

One major difference between the food habits of people and rats is that people are more influenced by the sensory appeal of foods. It is easier for people to overeat than rats. How food looks, smells, tastes, sounds, and feels in the mouth can influence people to overeat. Sweet foods or drinks and salty foods are easy for many to overconsume, and for some, they seem to be addictive.

In another experiment, twenty-three overweight subjects were given a choice between protein snacks and carbohydrate snacks. Most chose carbohydrates nearly all the time and had snack cravings at special times such as midafternoon or just before bed. The problem was not willpower but chemical imbalance. When these subjects were given a drug that raised serotonin levels, their snacking dropped dramatically.

I feel that the eating habits of most people, especially in the overeating of protein, fatty foods, and refined carbohydrates, have created abnormal conditions in the appetite center of the brain. Ordinary crash dieting simply produces further imbalances. The average fat intake per day in the United States is 40 to 50 percent of the daily food taken, twice as much as the amount recommended by the National Academy of Sciences. Getting back to a healthy, right way of eating is the ultimate solution to weight problems.

There is a correct way to take in fats. We can get all the fats we need when we use foods such as whole milk, eggs, avocados, nuts, nut butters, and other natural foods. Our bodies can handle and digest fats properly when they are a natural ingredient in foods. Concentrated fats and oils are much more difficult for the body to take care of.

HOW WE USE UP CALORIES

During a twenty-four-hour day, we burn up a certain number of calories, which varies according to what we do. Basal metabolism, the operation of all body functions in the resting state, takes about a calorie per minute, or 480 calories during an eight-hour sleep period. In our waking hours, exercise, household tasks, driving, job activities, walking, talking, and other normal aspects of life use up energy at varying rates. Calorie expenditures for a variety of activities are given in Table 3.2.

Surprisingly, perhaps, the major benefit of exercise is not in keeping the weight down by burning up fat but in keeping the appetite center normalized, moving the blood and lymph, toning and firming the muscles, and strengthening the heart. However, exercise does increase the metabolism for up to fifteen hours, and more fat is burned off. Research has shown that a combination of exercise and balanced diet is the very best way to reduce weight and keep it off. Fast weight loss just doesn't work over the long term. Patience is a key factor. Weight loss at a rate of one or two pounds a week allows the brain and body chemistry to rebalance and readjust, without triggering the "rebound effect" of gaining back all the old pounds.

Based on average activity levels for the average American, the following calorie charts have been worked out. Keep in mind that these figures are not intended to provide more than rough guidelines.

Calorie requirements vary considerably from individual to individual, but these charts will give you some idea of how many calories you normally need to get from your food to maintain a healthy weight.

HOW TO DETERMINE
YOUR IDEAL WEIGHT

Look at Table 3.3 on page 49 and find your ideal weight. For example, if you are a 5-foot, 2-inch female with a medium body frame, your ideal weight is 115 pounds (no matter what

Table 3.2. **Calories Burned per Hour for Various Activities**

Activity	Per Pound Ideal Weight	Activity	Per Pound Ideal Weight
Awake, reclining	0.50	Running (5.7 mph)	3.70
Bicycling	1.10	Sawing wood	3.12
Bookbinding	1.10	Sewing by hand	0.72
Carpentry	1.56	by machine	0.74
Dancing	1.95	Singing	0.79
Dishwashing	0.93	Sitting relaxed	0.65
Dressing/undressing	0.81	Skating	2.10
Driving car	0.88	Sleeping	0.43
Eating	0.65	Standing at attention	0.74
Exercise, light	1.10	relaxed	0.69
moderate	1.88	Stone masonry	2.60
strenuous	2.90	Sweeping	1.09
very strenuous	3.90	Swimming	3.25
Ironing	0.93	Tailoring	0.88
Knitting	0.73	Typing rapidly	0.91
Laundering	1.05	Walking downstairs	2.36
Painting	1.56	slowly	1.30
Peeling potatoes	0.75	moderately fast	1.95
Playing a cello	0.98	very fast	4.22
a piano	0.84	Walking up stairs	7.18
a violin	0.77	Writing	0.69
Ping-Pong	2.50	Vacuum cleaning	1.78
Reading aloud	0.69		

your real weight is). If you have gone out dancing for two hours and want to know how many calories you have used, simply multiply your ideal weight (115 pounds) by 1.95, the calories per hour used up per pound of ideal weight, as shown in Table 3.2, then multiply again by the number of hours—two. So, we have 115 × 1.95 × 2 = 448.5 calories. If you had only danced a half hour, it would be 115 × 1.95 × 0.5, or 112.1 calories.

Now, look up the ideal weight for your height, build, and sex. Consider whether it could reasonably be judged too high or too low for you. (It may be helpful to discuss this with your spouse.)

Decide on a weight goal that you can put your heart into achieving, and write it down on 3 × 5 cards or pieces of paper. Then put one on the wall in the bathroom, one in the kitchen, one in every room where you will see it relatively often and at strategic times of the day. These constant reminders of your goal will help you stick to it.

UNDESIRABLE FOODS TO AVOID

Your ultimate goal should be to find a healthy way of living where you won't need to diet. Plan on developing healthy eating habits so that your weight will stay where it is supposed to be. My diet plan is designed to help you do that, but it will not work unless you resolve to stay away from foods that are worthless or harmful to your health.

The following list of undesirable foods is not intended to be complete, but from it you can gain a clear understanding of what types of foods to leave alone. In general, all packaged foods and all foods containing chemical additives should not

Table 3.3. **Ideal Weight Chart**

Women				Men			
Height (without shoes)	Weight (without clothing) Body Frame			Height (without shoes)	Weight (without clothing) Body Frame		
	Sml	Med	Lg		Sml	Med	Lg
5 ft.	100	109	118	5 ft. 3 in.	118	129	141
5 ft. 1 in.	104	112	121	5 ft. 4 in.	122	133	145
5 ft. 2 in.	107	115	125	5 ft. 5 in.	126	137	149
5 ft. 3 in.	110	118	128	5 ft. 6 in.	130	142	155
5 ft. 4 in.	113	122	132	5 ft. 7 in.	134	147	161
5 ft. 5 in.	116	125	135	5 ft. 8 in.	139	151	166
5 ft. 6 in.	120	129	139	5 ft. 9 in.	143	155	170
5 ft. 7 in.	123	132	142	5 ft. 10 in.	147	159	174
5 ft. 8 in.	126	136	146	5 ft. 11 in.	150	163	178
5 ft. 9 in.	130	140	151	6 ft.	154	167	183
5 ft. 10 in.	133	144	156	6 ft. 1 in.	158	171	188
5 ft. 11 in.	137	148	161	6 ft. 2 in.	162	175	192
6 ft.	141	152	166	6 ft. 3 in.	165	178	195

be eaten because processing has robbed them of valuable nutrients and any added chemicals are a potential danger to health, no matter what the food industry says about their supposed safety. The best philosophy of eating is to stay with natural, whole, pure foods as closely as possible, most of them raw. Some vegetables and all grains and meats need to be cooked. We will get more into this later. Many frozen fruits and vegetables are all right, but some frozen products are processed or adulterated with chemicals, so read the labels.

Most people will stray from a good diet now and then, and it is not what we do once in a while that harms our bodies, so I do not take an extreme position on such things. But, you will find that as you eat more whole foods, you will lose the desire for many unnatural foods. Sweets will not have the same appeal. Fat-fried foods often become repulsive. Heavily salted snack foods will lose charm. While you are making the transition to a better diet, however, it is best not to have junk food in the house. Resist temptation by avoiding it altogether.

Ale	Chocolate
Any food substitute	Coffee
Beef jerky	Condensed milk
Beer	Cornstarch
Cakes, cookies, donuts, and pastries	Crackers (except sesame, Ak-Mak, etc.)
Candy	Dried fruit, sulfured
Canned food containing chemical additives	Dry packaged breakfast cereals (except muesli and whole grains)
Catsup	Egg substitutes
Chili	Fatty meats
Chips (potato, corn, etc.)	

French rolls and bread

Fried foods

Fruit, unripe

Fudge

Hard liquor

Highly seasoned foods

Hominy

Hot cakes

Ice cream

Lard

Macaroni

Malted milk

Marshmallows

Noodles

Packaged luncheon meats

Peanut butter

Pickles

Pies

Potatoes, peeled, mashed,
 or fried

Pork and beans

Pretzels

Puddings, packaged

Saccharin

Salt

Smoked meat, fowl, or fish

Soft drinks (including
 diet drinks)

Spaghetti

Sweet desserts

Sweetened or artificial
 fruit drinks

Syrup

Tapioca

Tea (not herbal)

White flour and products
 containing white flour

White rice

White sugar and products
 containing white sugar

The right way to count calories is to start with foods that count for health. Our digestive systems, appetite control centers, and body chemistry are designed to work properly with foods that are natural, whole, and pure. Adulterated foods, unripe foods, processed foods, man-made foods, and wrongly cooked foods tend to cause disturbances that eventually develop into serious health problems, vitamin and mineral deficiencies, and toxic settlements in the body. They also contribute generously to obesity.

One of the greatest aids I know in losing excess weight is raw foods. Have plenty of salads, using a variety of ingredients.

Use fresh fruits as desserts or between-meal snacks. Have carrots, celery, radishes, sliced cucumbers, tomatoes, bell pepper slices, or other raw vegetables you like in the refrigerator all the time to have with meals or between meals. There are few calories but many valuable nutrients in raw vegetables. Fruits have more vitamins but are higher in calories, so I advise only two a day as compared with six vegetables. I advise dropping wheat, milk, and sugar from your food regimen completely because most people have had so much of them that they have developed abnormal bodies.

CHAPTER 4

THINK RIGHT
TO KEEP FIT

One of the great paradoxes in life is that we must think right to have good health and we must have good health to think right. Thinking right, thinking vigorously, and the joyful feelings that come out of a mind that works effectively help balance the glandular system, especially the thyroid. While you are slimming down to a healthy weight, keeping in mind that you intend to stay there, resolve to change habits of thinking that may contribute to unwanted weight gain.

Here are some typical patterns of thinking that contribute to excess weight:

"I don't want to see these leftovers go to waste." (The economy excuse.)

"I've been so good today—got the kids off to school, finished the laundry and ironing, did the shopping—so I deserve a nice big piece of German chocolate cake." (The reward excuse.)

"I'm so mad (or frustrated or disappointed, etc.) at my wife (husband), I'm just going to have a big helping of cherry pie a la mode." (The revenge excuse.)

"Let's get out the cokes, chips, and popcorn—our favorite TV show is on." (The TV excuse.)

"It's three o'clock—time for my tea, toast, and jam." (The time excuse.)

"Aunt Helen's coming over, so we're going to have her favorite dessert—angel food cake and strawberry ice cream." (The visitor excuse.)

"The Hansens are such big eaters, we'd better have steak, potatoes, vegetables, salad, and dessert when they come to dinner." (The keep-up-with-the-Hansens excuse.)

"Surely, a few hors d'oeuvres won't hurt." (The little-bit-is-okay excuse.)

There are other habits of thinking that get us into trouble; we will discuss more of them later. The nice thing is, when we see our habits down on paper like this, we can laugh about them, then make a decision to change. While willpower isn't everything, without it, weight control is impossible, so let's realize a fact of life from the start: *Everybody Has Willpower.* All you have to do is learn to develop what you have and use it.

A DIET QUIZ

To assist in identifying areas of your life and thinking that may be obstacles to weight control for you, answer the following questions and think about your responses. There is no answer list to check your results; the object is simply to help you understand more about your food priorities and habits.

1. In comparison with other pleasures and satisfactions in your life, rate eating on a scale of one to ten.
2. In terms of your various priorities right now, rate being at the "right weight" on a scale of one to ten.
3. Can you think of more than two reasons why you would like to be slim?
4. Are you impatient to lose weight?
5. Do you consider dieting difficult or unpleasant?
6. Are you resentful toward yourself for being overweight?
7. Have you dieted before? How many times?
8. Do you look forward to getting off your diet so that you can eat certain foods you shouldn't have again?
9. Do you tend to eat more when you are fatigued?
10. How close to bedtime do you eat dinner? Is dinner your largest meal of the day?
11. Do you think other people find dieting easier than you do?
12. Do you have difficulty saying, "No, thank you," when someone offers you a drink or snack that you know is fattening?
13. Do you believe that thin people can eat all they want?
14. Are there foods you would go out in the evening to buy if you found you were out of them?
15. Are there friends of yours with whom your main pastime is eating?
16. If you have dieted before, was your main reason to appear more attractive, then you returned to your old lifestyle?
17. Before you read this book, were you aware that being overweight increased your chances of acquiring one or more diseases?
18. In terms of your other goals and priorities, rate being in good health on a scale of one to ten.

19. Is it hard for you to visualize yourself as a slim person?

20. If you have dieted before, did you continue to look into other reducing diets, diet pills, weight-loss methods, and so on?

21. Do you think about or fantasize about certain foods?

22. Can you think of one, two, or three foods that may be key foods in getting or keeping you overweight?

23. Do you have a hard time stopping once you've started eating them?

24. Do you tend to snack when you are bored or depressed?

25. Do you snack at certain times of the day? In certain rooms of the house or certain restaurants or coffee shops?

26. When you realize you have eaten more than you should during a single meal, do you continue to eat?

27. If you overeat at a couple of meals, do you give up on your diet and drop it?

28. Do you believe staying at the right weight would change your life in ways you would enjoy?

29. On a scale of one to ten, rate how difficult you believe staying at your right weight would be.

30. Have you ever considered that changing aspects of your lifestyle could make staying slim much easier?

Try to spend at least ten minutes reviewing and thinking about your answers. One of the keys to weight loss and better health is understanding your own life patterns, motivation, and personality.

MIND OVER "PLATTER"

Like it or not, our minds are married to our bodies, "for better or for worse." And it can be for better, as we learn to think our way to right living.

We have previously mentioned that the appetite center is located in a uniquely important part of the brain—the hypothalamus—which brings many mental faculties to bear on our eating habits. Both the thinking brain (cerebral cortex) and the emotional brain (limbic system) are linked to the hypothalamus—and, therefore, the appetite center—by important nerve channels. The hypothalamus also controls and monitors our endocrine glands, which dramatically affect how we think, feel, and behave. It does this via the pituitary gland, the "master gland" of the body.

We find that every thought, every feeling, affects every one of the billions of cells our bodies are made of. They do this by their effects on the nervous system and the glands. We must realize, if we are overweight, that our thoughts and emotions have contributed to the development of the problem in the first place and help maintain it in the second place—no matter what other causes there may be. A healthy, positive attitude and peace of mind toward both our present physical appearance and our future slender goals set us free to succeed in our goals.

There are a lot of people who gain weight when they stop smoking. Now, if a person has the willpower to stop smoking, he could use that willpower to stop eating so much and could fortify himself with a more balanced diet, foods that will not cause fat. Many of us eat from our feelings and not from our actual need for food. We find out when we feel good that we eat entirely differently than when we are morbid or depressed.

Overeating in a land of plenty such as the United States is not a subject so profound that we need to keep analyzing the situation. What is often abnormal, however, is what people do and think once the evidence of overeating is obvious to the individual and everyone else. Excess weight is a symptom that something is wrong with that person's body and lifestyle, just as symptoms of other chronic diseases are nature's way of telling us something is wrong. The right thing to do at that point is to remedy the situation, learn the lesson, and correct the problem. And the simple lesson in most cases of obesity is to eat less until weight normalizes, then stick to a balanced food plan such as my Health and Harmony Food Regimen.

CARE ENOUGH TO SAY "NO"

The first step in overcoming an undisciplined eating habit is to learn to say "no." One young lady allowed herself to get fat because she couldn't say "no" to aggressive men interested only in sex; getting fat solved that problem but made her unattractive, which she didn't like. When she learned to say "no" to men, she felt comfortable slimming down again.

It is not wrong to enjoy food. But it is not right to abuse our bodies through overeating, and this problem is not so difficult to correct. We have to put "mind over platter."

As we have said previously, some people eat when they are bored, depressed, nervous, anxious, or unloved. There are effective ways to deal with these problems, but eating is not one of them. When we believe that eating helps us feel better, then get disgusted when we see the fat that results, we are internalizing a mental conflict that invites a host of problems.

Discipline is not a gift or talent, it is a learned behavior that starts with an attitude of willingness to overcome. We can start to develop it by saying "no" in the case of small things in life, such as sleeping an extra ten minutes in the morning; a second cup of coffee with breakfast; an invitation to gossip or downgrade someone. Once you have experienced the power and authority of saying "no" to little things, go on to bigger and better things. Say "no" to second helpings. Say "no" to gravies. Say "no" to watching TV in the afternoon when you could be taking a walk. Say "yes" to things you know are good for your body, mind, and spirit. Discipline has its "yes" side, too.

Insecurity, low self-esteem, suppressed aggression, anger, resentment, bitterness, and other emotional disharmonies can manifest in overeating, possibly by causing imbalance in the appetite center as well as through purely psychological means, such as substitutional or compensatory behaviors.

People who aren't satisfied with their love and sex lives often turn to food. It is very important to have the sex life right so that substitutionary behaviors don't bring in some kind of imbalance. Foods, especially sweets, are among the most satisfying activities to most people, but we can't trade one thing for another and expect the body to stay in balance. The correction of lifestyle imbalance should be made in the original part of the lifestyle that was disturbed.

THINKING AND SPEAKING THINNESS

Some years ago, a major East Coast university conducted a survey of the words used by people in ordinary daily conversations and found that a high percentage of the average conversation was negative or critical. This, I believe, affects the body adversely.

Do you speak negatively about yourself? Do you think and speak critically of your own body, habits, characteristics, behavior, or abilities? Previously, we said that higher brain functions, such as thought, were connected to the part of the brain that houses the appetite center. I believe that the appetite center is affected by our speech and thoughts, and if we throw it out of balance, our eating habits can become abnormal and possibly the way our bodies digest, assimilate, and use nutrients as well.

Specifically, I want you to stop thinking and saying things like "I'm too fat," "I have a terrible weight problem," "I don't like the way I look," "All this flab looks terrible," "Everybody notices how fat I am," and "I feel miserable because of my weight." For each of these kinds of things you find yourself thinking or saying, substitute statements that indicate work or improvement, such as, "I feel better now that I'm doing something about my weight problem," or "I'm becoming slimmer every day."

Some years back, one of the popular weight control programs came up with the slogan, "Think thin." This is a wonderful idea. Think of yourself as thin. Think of your appetite as under control. Think of yourself as a person of authority who can say "no" to fattening food and drink, a person who can walk past a refrigerator without a second glance.

Ladies, imagine yourself in a lovely new dress, one or two sizes smaller. Men, imagine yourself in a good-looking suit with a leaner waistline by four or more inches. Picture these in your mind frequently to help build motivation. Some persons have actually gone to a department store and bought smaller-size dresses or suits in advance, then hung them in the closet to look at every day until they fit. And, of course, they do fit. The body follows the mind, the imagination, the will.

Can you see what we are getting at in this chapter? Can you see how what you think and say can be a wonderful, constructive help in shedding unwanted weight and staying as fit as you like? Learn to use language as a tool for accomplishing goals, such as losing a specific number of pounds and following a better lifestyle. Think in terms of success, of winning, of anticipating good results.

LOVE AS A REDUCING AID

As I have said before, many people who feel unloved overeat. Now, this is a serious problem because the person who feels unloved really doesn't care if he or she is overweight, and the heart of the problem here is not gluttony but loneliness. The problem is lack of a feeling of self-worth, of being lovable.

I have seen cases where feeling unloved produced glandular imbalance. The thyroid is the "emotional gland," very susceptible to emotional influence, and we find that an underactive thyroid can lead to unwanted weight gain even without overeating. We also find a loss of willpower and discipline when a person feels unloved. This is something we have to take care of. We need to be around people who love us for our own good. We have to leave old things behind and take on a new and better way of life.

In many cases of overweight problems, I have sensed that the excess weight was not going to leave until the person was willing to let go of something. It seemed as though the fat was being held in place by an unwillingness to change, to let go of the old and take on a new life. We can't hold on to grievances, bitter memories, and old problems without consequences to our bodies and our health.

WHAT ARE YOU CARRYING?

Is there a spiritual problem? Let go of it and make your peace with the Almighty. Are you resisting, resenting, and holding onto bad memories? Forgive the people involved. Do you feel unloved? Find someone who needs a friend and love him. You have to let go of the old and take on the new. Life is a flowing process; nothing is meant to stand still. Are you around mean, spiteful people? Find people who like you and leave the others behind.

The Good Book says, "Love your neighbor as yourself." My mother once taught me, "We have to love other people for our *own* good." Think about that. I don't say it's easy, but it's true. We can't love our neighbor unless we love ourselves, but maybe the key to loving ourselves is to show love to others first. Kindness is precious, and people appreciate it very much. Like love, it is one of those things that blesses those who give as well as those who receive. The best way of breaking out of the feeling of being unloved is to start doing something for other people. Love flowing through you is healing. You will soon feel loved.

Don't wait around for someone to bring love to you first. You take the first step.

Love is a healer because it releases those things in the mind that have grown stagnant and toxic. We can't love and feel bad at the same time. We can't love and hold onto bitter memories at the same time. Love triumphs over all obstacles. Love is always just right. And, in this sense, I believe love can be a reducing aid.

MOTIVATION AND REDUCING

Obviously you wouldn't be reading this book if you didn't have some degree of motivation to reduce your weight. But we find it is often helpful to examine our motivations, to check their consistency with our various goals in life. The basic question once again is, "Why do you want to lose weight?"

The reason we bring up the question is because many people *do not* want to lose weight. They want to appear attractive or athletic. They want to radiate sex appeal. They want to impress the boss, to increase chances of promotion. Or they want to lose enough weight so that they won't gain again when they get back to a normal food regimen. None of these people really wants to lose weight. They want something else, but they have to lose weight to get it.

Now, I don't think there is anything wrong with these things, but is there any reason you can't raise your sights a little and say, "I want to lose weight because I want to be as healthy as possible and to feel as wonderful as possible?" Stop and think about it. When you take the path to better health, all these other benefits come with it. You get a lot more than you get from a reducing diet, and it stays with you.

As I have said before, I believe the reason why 95 percent of all those who use reducing diets gain back the weight they lost within a year is because they go back to their old lifestyles.

What's wrong with the old lifestyle? It's too much to cover here, but I want to point out a few reasons why so many people's lifestyles are unhealthy in the United States: poor food choices, lack of exercise, too little fresh air and sunshine, staying up too late, excessive use of drugs and alcohol, chronic marital problems, too much rushing around, pollution, traffic, excessive noise, not enough sleep, not enough exposure to beauty, poor recreation choices, and other processes that contribute more to disease than to health.

What sense does it make to lose weight, then go back to a way of life dominated by other unhealthy factors? Why settle for one bite when you can have the whole apple?

Recheck your motivation: What do you really want out of life? How does good health fit into that context? What is being slimmer and feeling better going to do for you?

POSITIVE THOUGHTS FOR SUCCESSFUL REDUCING

Here are some mental exercises to do along with your diet, once you begin the program. Some call these "affirmations," others call them "autosuggestions" or "meditations."

Sit in a comfortable chair in a quiet room where you will not be disturbed for ten to fifteen minutes. Do three of the following exercises each day; if you learn them by heart and do them from memory, so much the better. Say each one alternately aloud and silently to yourself at least six times.

1. Love

I allow love to flow into and flow out of myself, carrying away every obstacle to being a fully loving and lovable person. I will be loving toward others and toward myself, allowing my body to become healthier, stronger, and slimmer, day by day.

2. Authority

I have complete authority over everything I take in at the spiritual, mental, and physical levels. I choose to think positive thoughts and select the right foods to make my mind clear and to help my body reach its natural weight. I can say "no" to any fattening food and "yes" to any food that is right for my body. I am in charge of choosing the times and places I will eat. I have authority over myself.

3. Enjoyment

I enjoy my life right now, delighting in the foods I eat, glad that I am not eating foods that put on weight, glad that I am losing weight each day. I enjoy the feeling of my body as I become more fit and slimmer, and I am thankful that changes are being made for the better in my body and mind.

4. Letting Go of the Old

I choose to let go of the old and become a new person. I choose to release any old memory that hinders my progress toward reaching my natural, healthy weight. I choose to release any old habit that has contributed to my weight problem in the past. The old has passed out of my life, and I welcome the new.

5. Thankfulness

I am thankful for each new day, thankful for the many wonderful things in my life, and thankful for friends and loved ones. I am thankful for my health and for my peace of mind. I am thankful that my mind molds to a new way when I put the right thoughts in it. I am thankful that every day, in every way, I am succeeding in reaching my weight goal.

6. Self-Discipline

I am completely in charge of my body and its needs, and I realize my body follows the leading of my mind. I have complete confidence that by means of correct self-discipline, my body will mold to a better, healthier, slimmer way of life. Because self-discipline is a form of love, a way of taking responsibility for my own looks, actions, and health, I gladly open myself to receive the many blessings I expect from it: self-confidence, self-respect, self-control, peace of mind, and greater enjoyment of life.

7. Serenity

My nerves are strong and calm, stronger and calmer, stronger and calmer than ever before. I feel in harmony with myself, with the universe, and with everything around me. I am rich with inner powers that give me harmony, security, and serenity, that give me the ability to comfortably, easily, and gracefully lose weight. Nothing and nobody can bring me out of unity with the Higher Powers that protect me, and I am rich with inner powers that give me harmony, security, and serenity, that give me the ability to comfortably, easily, and gracefully lose weight. Nothing and nobody can bring me out of unity with the Higher Powers that protect me and make me invincible, invulnerable, and unshakable.

8. Vitality

I feel full of health and the joy of living. There is sunshine in my soul today. The clouds have rolled away, and I feel confident, reassured, and ever so contented. I feel young, ever so young. Every day in every way I feel my normal weight developing and a return of more vitality. As each pound of fat melts away, I grow more energetic, more filled with vitality. I use this vitality to burn up calories. I feel like a new and powerful personality, able to overcome any obstacle with the greatest of ease. I feel wonderful—simply marvelous.

9. Slenderness

Every day in every way I am growing more fit and slim. Every day in every way I am feeling better and better. Every day in every way I am growing closer to my ideal weight, to the weight natural to my body. I love my body. I am at peace with myself and I know I am on the right path.

FINAL SUGGESTIONS

Don't talk a lot about your diet, but on every appropriate occasion, simply tell friends and others, "I feel wonderful! I am making changes for the better all the time."

When you find yourself thinking or daydreaming about food, change your thoughts or dreams to a beautiful natural scene, such as a mountain lake or stream, or to an activity you enjoy, such as roller skating, doing crossword puzzles, hiking, bird watching, going to an art gallery, or whatever else you like.

Two of the greatest obstacles to success in weight loss and weight management are excuses and blaming others. When you can let go of these things and begin to take responsibility for your own life, important and wonderful changes will begin to take place. I can't tell you how valuable it is to be responsible for your own life.

One of the greatest encouragements toward succeeding in your weight-loss goal is to put a picture on the wall showing your ideal shape. This inspires the conscious mind and provides a nonverbal incentive for the unconscious mind.

CHAPTER 5

EXERCISE KEEPS US TRIM

Exercise isn't the easiest way to turn a person on, especially if he is busy. Busy people seem to put exercise aside, hoping that they will be able to keep the nice lithe figure that came as a free gift with youth. But there comes a time, either in middle age or, if we've been eating too much and sitting around too often, when we suddenly realize we have developed bulges in the wrong places. We develop padding over our thighs, rear ends, and stomachs that is really difficult to get off. Seldom is anyone overjoyed at this discovery.

Of course, prevention of excess weight is best, because losing weight is very difficult to do. I think people develop self-defeating philosophies about prevention. *Why should I try to prevent something I don't have?* they ask. Weight goes on easily— and very subversively—over a long period of time. We don't notice the little quarter-inch bulge that appeared at first, but six months later, it's up to half an inch and six months more it's up to an inch. Then our best friend says something like, "Aren't you putting on a little weight?" Your belt doesn't take the same notch it used to, or your pants don't fit the same, and you have to let them out or get new ones. Of course, this book wasn't written for those who do not need to reduce, but I think it would be appropriate if we realized that some of the principles laid down in this book are for keeping us at a proper weight.

Music is a great stimulant in getting us to exercise. It virtually leads us into movement, creating such enjoyment that it takes the work out of exercise, or seems to, anyway. Be sure to try exercising to music.

To get the most from exercise, we should do it daily. Anyone who exercises three times a week will get good results from it. Those who exercise five days a week will get three times as much good out of exercising only two days more. We have presented here many more exercises than you can do, so you can select the ones that are right for your particular program and you can change to get more variety when you are tired of one set of exercises.

A good exercise program circulates the blood into the fat tissues to dissolve the fat and to bring it back into the blood to be broken down and eliminated.

When we stop and think about it, the more weight we gain, the less physical activity and exercise we tend to do. We can turn that statement around, and it is just as true. The less physical activity and exercise we tend to do, the more weight we gain. It's as simple as that.

Exercise alone, as we have said before, is not the best way to lose weight. For example, running a mile at a pretty good clip will only burn up 120 calories, less than an ounce of fat. This can be somewhat discouraging, unless we add up all the benefits of exercise.

∞ **Average Weight Gain**

The average American gains a pound a year after age twenty-five, according to Dr. Jack Wilmore, physical education expert at the University of Arizona.

First, however, no one who is over forty years old or more than 10 pounds overweight should begin an exercise program without consulting a doctor. Similarly, if you have a heart condition, ulcers, or any other serious physical problem, you should see a doctor about what exercises you can do. You should also tell the doctor about the diet plan you are on when you ask his advice concerning exercise.

It is not our purpose here to present a universal exercise plan since exercise needs vary according to age, sex, state of health, and amount of excess weight. What I want to do is show you what the benefits of exercise are, and how they fit into the kind of natural lifestyle where we look and feel our best. The human body is designed by nature to work best when we get adequate exercise and rest. Every organ responds to exercise and proper nutrition.

HOW EXERCISE KEEPS WEIGHT DOWN

What most people don't understand is that the whole body is affected by obesity (and by weight loss). Exercise is one of the necessary ingredients for everyone's health, not just overweight people, but it is nice to know that a physically fit body burns fat calories faster, easier, and more safely than a soft, flabby body. Permanent weight control, based on a right way of living, must include exercise.

Possibly the most interesting fact about exercise is that twenty to thirty minutes of vigorous activity once each day causes the basal metabolism to rise and stay up (above normal) for nearly fifteen hours after exercising! This means that your body is burning up calories faster than usual as you go through your normal day's work and activity, or even as you sleep. This is a bonus in speeding up weight loss.

Second, exercise tones the bowel and promotes regularity, which assists in weight loss. Studies have shown that the longer wastes remain in the bowel, the more cholesterol is absorbed back into the body. Where is this extra cholesterol stored? Mostly in fat cells.

Third, we need to exercise to move the blood and lymph, stimulating good blood circulation to the brain to ensure this vital organ gets all the nutrients it needs, and moving the lymph along to get rid of bacteria, foreign matter, and wastes. The blood and lymph carry off the breakdown products of fat catabolism, assisting in the weight-loss process. But we must realize the lymph system has no "heart" to act as a pump as the blood circulatory system does; the lymph system consists of the spleen, thymus, appendix, tonsils, lymph vessels, lymph nodes, and fluid. Muscle movement is the only thing that moves lymph. So exercise is vital to the lymph circulation and in getting enough blood to the brain. The latter is particularly important because without a sufficient blood supply, the brain would become deficient in needed nutrients and would gradually lose its efficiency in running the heart, lungs, kidneys, liver, and so on, as well as in regulating weight.

The heart muscle is strengthened by exercise. This is important because each pound of fat, so it is said, has several miles of

---

∞ **Lymphatic System**

Foods: Green, leafy vegetables, watercress, celery, okra, apples.

Drinks: Potato peeling broth, celery juice, blue violet tea, parsley juice, carrot juice, apple juice.

Vitamins: A, C, choline, B-complex, B_1, B_2, B_6, biotin, pantothentic acid, folic acid.

Minerals: Potassium, chlorine, sodium.

Herbs: Blue violet tea (leaves), chaparral, burdock, echinacea, blue flag, poke root, goldenseal, cayenne, mullein, black walnut. (Best taken in extract form if available.)

---

blood vessels and capillaries running through it, which create an extra burden on the heart. Strengthening the heart helps compensate for the stress placed on it by obesity, even as excess weight is being burned away.

The aerobic aspect of exercise promotes efficient oxygenation of the blood in the lungs and efficient removal of carbon dioxide. Oxygen is needed to break down the fats and lipids in the body in the process of energy conversion.

Perspiration during exercise gets rid of acids and toxic wastes near the skin surface and keeps the pores open for elimination. The skin is an elimination organ, a "third kidney" so to speak, which helps keep the body free of toxic accumulations. Toxins in tissues lower the metabolic rate and slow down the process of getting rid of fat.

Finally, some experts say that exercise depresses the appetite center, actually helping to control the urge to overeat. Possibly this is due to the more efficient digestion and assimilation that exercise stimulates, resulting in a lowered need and desire for food.

BEST FORMS OF EXERCISE

Walking briskly is the best all-around exercise, while swimming is the best exercise for those with back trouble. There are, however, many forms of exercise that are not suitable for overweight people, especially those who are 50 pounds or more over their ideal weight. We will present some special exercises for people with this condition.

Exercise should be regular, building up to at least thirty minutes a day, preferably at the same time each day, strenuous enough to bring the pulse rate up, accelerate and deepen the breathing, and bring on a light perspiration. For those who are 40 pounds or more overweight or those in poor physical condition, I recommend starting with no more than ten minutes per day for the first two weeks, using easy stretching and bending exercises to get the body limber and to flex the joints. Don't strain and don't attempt to reach the perspiration point at first. Walking can be substituted. Walk four blocks or so each day the first three days and add two more blocks every three days until you are walking for a total of thirty minutes. Then gradually increase the briskness of your walk until you are walking the same distance faster each day. Swimming can be substituted in a similar program. Start slow and easy, then gradually build up in speed and distance.

Horseback riding is very good for those who are in a position to do it once a week for an hour or so. Every muscle in the body is stimulated by the movement of the horse. The bowel and internal organs are flexed and toned, and the entire body is well oxygenated, which helps burn off fat calories. Keep in mind that horseback riding, or any other once-a-week form of exercise, should only be used along with a daily exercise program. We do not get enough good from exercising once a week.

Fitness programs at health clubs are fine for some people but not for others. They can be very time consuming, considering the two-way drive and showering afterward, but if you are one of those who benefits from exercising with a group and are highly motivated by it, check it out with your doctor. I think many of the spa programs are beneficial, especially under supervision.

Be sure the kind of exercise you choose, the amount of time involved, and the equipment, if any, will fit into your daily routine well enough to keep you motivated. The more you enjoy your exercise, the more likely you are to keep it up. Remember, music helps make exercise fun.

By equipment, I am referring to the various things you can buy at sporting goods stores, department stores, and through some health food stores. These include indoor bicycle exercisers, bouncers that look like mini-trampolines, treadmills, and gadgets with elastic bands to pull against. These can be very good, but make sure the equipment you choose is right for you before you buy.

You should always start with warmup exercises, such as simple stretches and bends, before getting into the active exercises. There are all kinds and degrees of aerobics. Some are quite strenuous. So I want you to take it easy at first. Increase your efforts over a period of time; be good to your body.

A MUSICAL NOTE

Women, especially, love to exercise to music. Men do, too, but I believe women are drawn more to dance by their natures. Women may be more deeply moved by music. So I urge those who select exercises from the ideas in this chapter to do them to music for greater benefits and higher motivation.

Music adds another dimension to exercise. No one can sit still when lively music is played. The feet tap, the legs move, the fingers snap, and the whole body gets into the rhythm and the spirit. One of the finest compilations to use with beginner-level exercise is *Hooked on Swing.* It is relatively slow and it moves nicely. *Hooked on Classics* and *Hooked on Disco* are also good accompaniments to exercise.

We find that the heavier person can do exercises to music with a slower beat (but not too slow) quite comfortably and enjoyably on a bouncer or rebounder (as the mini-trampoline is sometimes called). I will describe some rebounder exercises you can do to music right after the section on stretching, twisting, and bending exercises on page 80. If you start out slowly and carefully, it is not necessary to do any warmup exercises before getting on the bouncer because you will be warming up on it before getting into the more active side of exercising.

After your *skin brushing,* described below, I recommend that you start with figure eight exercises and a little stretching and bending for five minutes twice each day—before breakfast and before the evening meal. Gradually work up to a half hour of these exercises before changing to others. Don't let yourself get completely out of breath. Exercise only until you are feeling warm and perspiring lightly.

SKIN BRUSHING

I call the skin "the third kidney" because of its importance in eliminating acid wastes from the body. The skin is a living organ with blood and lymph vessels, nerves, oil glands, and small muscles surrounding each hair and pore. Because dead skin cells build up on the skin, and because the muscles under the skin need stimulation, I recommend skin brushing as a method of stimulating, toning, and cleansing that is not adequately done in taking a bath or shower. Skin brushing aids reducing by increasing the rate of elimination.

Skin Brushing Exercise

Using a long-handled vegetable bristle brush (not nylon bristles), scrub the body from neck to feet twice a day for about five minutes each time, as vigorously as is comfortable for you. Those who have very sensitive skin will have to go a little lighter on the brushing than others. Women should avoid brushing the breasts, and both sexes should use a softer brush on the face where the skin is more sensitive. We need to keep the skin active and stimulated. Brushing is done in any direction with a dry brush. We make new skin cells every twenty-four hours and skin brushing is essential for healthy skin and active elimination.

FIGURE EIGHT EXERCISE SYSTEM FOR THE JOINTS

Fitness experts have a saying that goes "use it or lose it," and nowhere does this apply better than to the flexibility of the joints. We have to use them to keep them limber. There is another saying: "You are as young as your joints," which is something to think about. What can a person do once the joints become stiff?

We must have limber joints. If your joints are stiff now, you may have calcium deposits, so be careful. The diet I present at the end of the book, and my Health and Harmony Food

Regimen, which is to be used after you have reached your weight-loss goal, will gradually bring any calcium deposits or spurs back into solution in the bloodstream. Meanwhile, go easy on the exercises, because moving the joints too much when there are calcium deposits may irritate the joints.

All figure eight exercises follow a circle pattern. The reason calcium spurs develop sometimes is because we don't use circular motion enough. When we walk or jog, our joints move back and forth, not around and around as they should. Figure eights are *corrective exercises* and should be done every day.

You should understand by now that our weight-loss program in this book is designed to improve your health as you exercise and follow your diet. The two—diet and exercise— work together in *natural harmony*. Exercise without a proper diet is not wise. Our reducing plan is designed to work in harmony with nature, and this is not what most diet plans do.

The Figure Eight Exercise System is the best way I know to keep the joints limber and flexible. The exercises are carefully thought out and put together so that you can get the greatest amount of good from them. We can also bring these exercises onto the bouncer if we want to do so. These exercises move the blood and lymph in the joint areas. They have been used by dancers for many years, and they will work just as well for you. Most people find them fun to do, especially to music. Repeat each exercise three to six times.

Knee Joints

Move the knee joints in a circular motion by bending the knees slightly, moving in circles or "figure eight" motions in each direction. Work up to ten times each day (placing the hands on the knees for balance is helpful). This knee exercise uses all sides of the joints not normally used, and keeps them pliable, limber, and supple.

Hip Joints

Stand with your feet 6 to 8 inches apart and visualize a figure eight on the floor. Stand in the center of the "8" and move the hips and buttocks in circular or figure eight motions in each direction. Make the figure eight motion as large as possible to the left and right sides. It is almost like the hula dance movement.

Shoulder Joints

Visualize a figure eight around your shoulders. Move your shoulders in figure eight motions in each direction. Lead with the right and then the left shoulder. Work up to ten times in each direction.

Neck

This exercise is similar to the ancient Persian dance "neck loops." Look straight ahead. Do not look to either side. Slide the head straight over to the right side in a figure eight or circular motion. The neck is over the shoulders, so to speak, a different movement than used in everyday movements and in different directions. Keep your eyes and head looking straight ahead.

STRETCHING, TWISTING, AND BENDING EXERCISES

Simple stretching, twisting, and bending exercises can be done by anyone who does not have back problems. I will describe a few here to help get you started. Move slowly and gracefully, staying within the comfort zone with respect to how far you twist or bend and how much you stretch.

Floor Touching

Raise both arms over your head and, bending at the waist, reach your hands toward your toes. If you are very heavy, this bend may seem more like a partial bow to a king, but don't push it. Only go as far as you can, ten times. The eventual object is to be able to touch your toes on the floor without bending the knees.

Airplane Twist

Hold both arms straight out to the side like airplane wings. Keeping them straight, rotate right and left from the waist, twisting only as far as is comfortable. Do this ten times.

Sky-Reach

Hold both arms straight up again. Pretend you are trying to grasp something above your head, just out of reach. You don't need to look up, just reach as high as you can, coming up on your tiptoes to reach a little higher. Breathe in with each stretch upward, exhale with each relaxation, coming down from tiptoe position but with the arms still extended up. Do ten times.

Stretch-Reach

Alternate arm stretches are a variant of the previous exercise, using somewhat different muscles. In this exercise, raise both arms over the head again, but keep both feet flat on the floor. On an inward breath, stretch only the right arm upward, holding the spine as straight as possible, then exhaling as you bring the right arm back. Do the same with the left arm and continue alternating, ten times each side.

Down-Stretch

Another side-stretching exercise starts by placing the right hand on the right hip, elbow out to the side, with the left arm straight down the left side, fingers extended. Carefully and gently extend the left hand down as far on the left leg as you can comfortably go. Don't try to overreach. Do ten times on the left, then ten times on the right.

Hip Rotation

Put both hands on your hips. Holding the upper body straight and the legs straight together, rotate at the waist in a circular motion five times around to the left, then five times around to the right.

Dive Stretch

Spread your feet about 2 feet apart and bring your hands together above your head with as little elbow bend as possible, like a diver about to go off the diving board on a straight dive. Bending and rotating slightly at the waist at the same time, point the hands (together) first at the right foot, then between the two feet, then at the left foot, then swing back to the starting position to the count of four. Don't try to bend or stretch to the point of discomfort. Eventually, you will be able to touch your toes and the floor, but possibly not at first. Repeat ten times.

Variation: Stand with your knees slightly bent and feet

3 feet apart. Raise your arms overhead, and place your hands together as if to dive into a pool. Bend over slowly from the hips, allowing the knees to bend, too, and reach as far back through your legs as possible. Swing back into an upright position, arms overhead again. Start slowly, and increase speed as you go along (ten times).

Half Squat

With hands on your hips, back erect, lower the buttocks about halfway to the knees, then come up again, breathing out on the down move, in on the up move. Do not attempt to go into a full squatting position. Halfway is sufficient. Repeat ten times.

CHAIR EXERCISE SYSTEM: MORE STRETCHING AND BENDING

As in the case of the other exercises, these are more fun done to music. The only difference here is that you will be using a chair to help keep your balance while you do more stretching and bending.

Side-Kick

Place both hands on the chair back, stand behind the chair with feet together, keeping toes pointed; kick leg sideways (actually, this is more a quick leg "raise" than kick), bring it back, and continue ten times. Repeat with the right leg. Raise the legs as high to the side as you can.

Stretch and Shift

All these exercises (with the exception of the last one) use the same position of hands on the chair back, so I will not keep repeating it. Spreading the feet about 3 feet apart, point the toes outward, and get into a semi-squat position. Now shift to the left so that the left knee bends more and more, while the right leg goes into a straight stretch. Reverse, then go to the other side, bending the right knee and straightening the left leg (ten times).

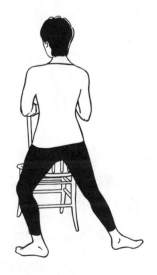

Backward Leg Lift

Again, use the chair to help keep your balance (place one hand or forearm on the back of the chair and the other hand on the chair seat), placing your feet about 2 feet away. Kick the leg (on the same side as the hand on the chair seat) up and out without tilting your hips. Keep the other foot flat on the floor. Do ten repetitions. Then repeat with the other leg, switching hand positions on the chair.

Leg-Lift, Foot-Hold

Stand behind the chair as in the side-kick exercise. With your left hand on the chair back, lift the right knee as close to your chest as possible. Balancing on the other foot, clasp your right ankle or foot in the right hand. Then bending toward the chair, move the right knee under the body, lifting the leg as high as you can while still holding the ankle or foot. Flex the muscle of the leg, pushing against the hand and trying to straighten the knee.

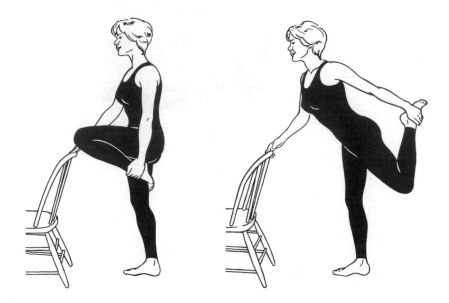

The benefit of all exercise is realized through rest. Always rest for at least ten minutes after exercising, either lying down or sitting in a comfortable chair. A cup of Cleavers tea, also known as goose grass tea, may be appropriate at this time because it stimulates perspiration, aids circulation, and soothes the urinary system.

REBOUNDER EXERCISE SYSTEM TO MUSIC

Rebounder exercises to music introduce a level and type of physical activity that most people can take. Three to five minutes on the rebounder is equal to a mile of jogging, and every muscle in the body is exercised without subjecting the joints or bony structures to the sudden impact shock that takes place when running or jumping on a hard surface.

Many years ago, after visiting an osteopath in Hawaii who had a full-sized trampoline in his backyard, I designed a mini-trampoline for use by my patients long before the bouncers and rebounders so popular today were available.

We had a policeman at the Ranch who was on an early retirement due to an intervertebral disk problem that affected his back and neck, giving him a great deal of pain. I started him out on the bouncer with very easy exercises, with gentle movements. He could do them without any problem, although he felt a little pain the day after his exercises. With my encouragement, he persisted and gradually increased the time and vigor of his exercises more and more. In a few weeks, his problem was corrected. This is what got me started on the rebounder exercises and showing my patients how to do them.

Rebounder exercises are actually tension-relaxation exercises. Our bodies tense as our feet land on the flexible cover of the rebounder and relax as we go into the air. This is what does our bodies so much good. The routine on the bouncer is a very important part of my own exercise regimen, and I enjoy this very much, always bouncing to music.

We must be kind to our joints. The great thing about these rebounder exercises is that they are easy on the material that makes up the joints, and this is very important. Many exercises are harsh and jolting to the joints, compressing and stretching the soft inner material too much.

We must be kind to our joints because it is said that you are as young as your joints, and if they have been abused or if the diet is out of balance, they can become stiff, inflamed, and painful.

The soft inner material of the joints is extremely sensitive to the acid/alkaline balance of the blood. If the blood is too acid, calcium spurs may develop. We must realize that incorrect diet and overexercise are harmful to the joint material.

Our exercises should never be so strenuous or overdone that more acids are produced than our diets and elimination channels can take care of, or the joints will be affected. We should never go beyond what our bodies can handle or we will find out that there are consequences to our health. For this reason, diet and exercise should be well harmonized.

You can use any music you like, but make sure the rhythm and tempo increase through the first three songs or pieces you choose. It is best to record these three tunes on tape to run consecutively, so you can just turn on your tape recorder in the morning and get right into it. The time is about ten minutes for three pieces of music. You can increase the length of the music if you wish by adding other tunes later, after you are used to the ten-minute starting program given here.

There are more than one set of exercises. Learn one—do it, then learn another and do that one. Then you can do two, three, four, or five combinations. Your daily exercise routine shouldn't take longer than half an hour.

BOUNCER

The main purpose of these exercises is to move the lymph and carry off the broken-down products of metabolism. These movements firm the buttocks, help reduce the waist, and strengthen the legs. Be inventive. Make up some of your own dance movements as you go along. The object is to use as many muscles as possible and to move as many of the joints as possible.

Turn on your music!

Hands

Moving the feet in time with the music, let your body sway while flexing your fingers and hands with your arms above your head, down at your sides, extended like airplane wings, out in front of your body, and behind your back. Work those fingers in time with the music in quick, flexing movements to exercise all the little muscles. You can continue the hand exercises in some of the other bouncer exercises, if you choose.

Toes and Ankles

Lift up on your toes, and then swing your heels in and out (toward one another, away from one another). Then bring the heels down and swing the knees (held closely parallel) in circles to the left and to the right.

Knees

As you do these exercises, bend and straighten your knees. Flex those knees, not by removing your feet from the bouncer but by "jogging" gently from the knees only.

Hula Hips

Move your hips in a circular motion, then side to side, then front to back (thrusting your pelvis forward, then drawing it back), several times with each motion. Move your arms in graceful hulalike motions, keeping your hands parallel, rolling your shoulders to work the upper body. Add in the knee movements and the hand flexes.

Shoulder Rolls

Drop the hands to your sides and rotate the shoulders alternately, left shoulder, then right shoulder, then repeat; rotate your shoulders in forward circles several times, then reverse circles, then do both shoulders at the same time, forward and reverse. Keep the legs going, the knees flexing, and the hips swaying as you do this.

Swimming

Make swimming motions with your arms while keeping your feet, knees, and hips moving—move the body continuously.

Twist and Bend

Twist your body from side to side several times; bend your body slightly forward, then slightly backward several times.

Neck Rolls

Move your neck from side to side, then front to back, like a dancer. Rotate your hips in circles, then the knees and the arms.

Eyes

Hold the head still and make wide circles in the air in front of you, first with one hand, then the other, following your hands with your eyes. Repeat, closing the fist and making circles with one finger, following the finger with the eyes as you trace large circles clockwise, then counterclockwise, first with one hand, then the other. Repeat six times each way. Then turn on the bouncer until you are squarely facing one wall. Again, holding the neck and head still, look from the upper right corner of the wall you are facing to the lower left corner, *moving the eyes only.* Shift the eyes to the upper left corner, then to the lower right. Repeat six times. Then shift the eyes to the right and do the same thing.

Figure Eight Exercises

The bouncer is a fine place to do the figure eight exercises, and you may want to use them as part of your bouncer routine instead of doing them separately.

As the music shifts to the second tune, repeat the preceding exercises to the faster beat without lifting your feet from the bouncer. Do shoulder and arm movements like Fred Astaire and Ginger Rogers when they danced, especially the figure eights with the arms and shoulders (see shoulder joints illustration on page 79).

Move your hands and arms in hulalike motions again. Move those feet! Repeat all hand and arm movements in the first four exercises. Move the hands in large circles in front of your face, one hand at a time, keeping your eyes on your hands without moving the neck. Make clockwise and counterclockwise circles. Keep moving in time to the music.

By the time the third and fastest piece of music comes on, you'll be warmed up enough to increase your activity level. When you increase the amount of time you spend on the rebounder, use it on this faster beat since you don't need any more of the warmups. Later, when you are able to use your rebounder to its limit, the more active exercise will increase your basal metabolism and continue to burn up calories all day.

Repeat the movements as described in the first part of this section, but vary the foot movements.

Knee Crossover

Cross the right knee over the left and bring it back. Then cross the left knee over the right. Repeat six times, alternating.

Pigeon-Penguin

With toes pointed together and heels apart, bounce. Then bring heels together and toes apart and bounce. Repeat six times, alternating.

Kicks

Kick one foot forward, then the other. When you kick, reach down toward the toes of the kicking foot with one hand. Repeat six times.

Belly Up-Belly Down

As you bounce up, bring both hands to the lower-left abdomen and lift your belly a little as you go up and down, about six times. Then move the hands to the lower-right abdomen and repeat, again, holding up the middle of the abdomen. You can do this with high jumps if you are comfortable in the process.

Arm Circles

Bend at the waist and swing your arms from side to side in unison while bouncing on the mini-trampoline.

Jump Kicks (Goose Step)

This exercise helps to develop your balance. Kick each leg forward as if running, bouncing with each kick.

The Elephant

Clasp the hands, bend slightly forward, and with the feet apart, swing both arms to the left, then to the right, just as an elephant swings its trunk from side to side. The movement should be a graceful but energetic arms-and-shoulders stretch to one side, then the other.

After you get used to these, dream up your own bouncer routine with any movements you like, including dance movements. Be creative. Just be aware of the flexibility and limited foot space of the bouncer. I can't possibly mention all the fun exercises you can do on a bouncer, but I want to encourage you to make up some of your own exercises and have a good time with your bouncer!

If you are thirsty after exercising, add a crushed watercress tablet to your water or take an organic potassium tablet, so your body will not hold liquid. This is especially important for those lymphatic types who retain water easily. Also, you may wish to take vitamin B_6, which has been recommended by health researchers to help keep the water down in the body. Do not take more than 500 milligrams per day without talking to your doctor about it.

There are plastic suits you can buy to increase perspiration while you exercise and afterward. Ask your doctor about this, since for some this may not be a safe procedure. Perspiration is good for elimination of subcutaneous toxic material, but too much liquid loss can upset the chemical balance of the body.

FLOOR EXERCISE SYSTEM

There are many good toning exercises that can be done lying down, but they are only for people who are able to get down and up from the floor without strain. If you are too heavy to safely do exercises on the floor, wait until you have shed enough pounds to do these more conveniently. Use other exercises until you are able to get down on the floor and back up without difficulty.

Simple Abdomen Stretch

Lying on your back, start with your arms at your sides and lift them fully over your head, slowly, until they are flat on the floor above the head. Leave them there for a count of ten, then bring them back to the sides and start over. Do ten repetitions.

Rubber Ball Exercise

Lying on your back, head down on a slant board, or on the floor, roll a ball about the size of a tennis ball around on your abdomen with the palm of your hand. Use enough force so that you can really feel it. This tones the bowel. Note any sore spots, and spend more time rolling the ball over them. Like all slant board exercises, this one is particularly good for prolapse of the transverse colon.

Knee Flex

Lying on your back, draw your left knee as close to your chest as possible while breathing in, then return it to the floor while breathing out. Repeat with the right leg. Do ten repetitions with each leg.

Knee Crossover, Hip Roll

Do this one only if you don't have to strain. Lying on your back, bend your right knee and bring it over your left leg, rolling over partly on your left hip, while keeping your back on the floor and your arms at your sides, palms down to hold the position. Only go as far as you can without straining, and do not roll over onto your left side. Bring the right leg back to the floor, then repeat with the left leg and the right hip. Do five repetitions with each leg for the first week, then work your way up to ten the second week.

Neck Lift

Lying on your back, try lifting your head slightly from the floor, tipping your chin toward your chest. Do not strain to do this. If you can't get your head off the floor at first, simply tense the muscles as if trying to do it, then relax. After a week, you should be able to get your head off the floor at least a little. Keep practicing. Start with five repetitions for the first week; work up to ten by the end of the second week.

Full Hip Rolls

Lying on your back, put your arms out airplane style, palms to the floor for stability. Bring your knees up as high as possible. Keeping the knees bent and together, roll them to the left as far as you can without straining. Bring them back. Repeat on the right side. Start with five repetitions the first week and work up to ten the second week.

Abdominal Squeeze

Lying on your back, raise your knees, keeping your feet flat on the floor. Knees should be touching. Take a breath and squeeze your knees together for the count of three, then relax. Repeat for a total of ten repetitions.

Pelvic Lifts

With your knees up and your feet on the floor, as in the previous exercise, press your lower back onto the floor while trying to lift and tighten your buttocks. Don't strain and don't try to lift your back up. If you don't get off the floor at first, don't worry. It will come. Squeeze your buttocks together as you lift. Start with five repetitions, and work up to ten by the end of the second week.

Side Leg Lifts

Roll onto your right side, get up on your right elbow and forearm, and bend your right leg into an "L" at the knee for stability. Leave the top (left) leg straight, point the toes, and try to lift your leg level with your hip, or as high as is comfortable. Hold for a count of three, then let down and relax. Do this with both legs five times. Each week add another count, until you can hold each leg up for a count of seven.

More Leg Lifts

With your face and stomach down on the floor, lift one leg about 4 to 6 inches off the floor, hold briefly, then bring it down and repeat with the other leg. Inhale on the lift, exhale as you bring the leg down. Do four the first day, then add one more each day for each leg. If you can't get your legs off the floor at first, simply lift until you feel strain, then relax.

Heel Kicks

Again, lying face down on the floor, kick your heels back, one at a time, and try to touch your buttocks. Do five repetitions on each side.

SLANT BOARD EXERCISE SYSTEM

Many times we don't realize that the body is underactive and overweight partly because the brain is not getting the proper blood circulation. This is extremely important because the brain is the symphony conductor that directs the activity of every organ, gland, and tissue in the body, and if the brain is not fed right, the whole body suffers. The quickening force for every organ of the body comes from the brain, but people whose occupations cause them to sit or stand continually are sometimes unable to get the blood to the brain tissues because of inactive circulation and the counterforce of gravity. Problems frequently arising are prolapse of the transverse colon or pro- lapsed uterus (prolapsed means "dropped").

Slant boards can be purchased at many sporting goods stores and department stores, or they can be constructed by any "do-it-yourselfer." Basically, they consist of a padded board with a strap at one end to hold the ankles.

The slant board is the best exercise for getting blood to the head, for drawing a prolapsed colon into place, for rectal and prostate conditions, for uterine pressure problems, for improv- ing circulation to the pelvic organs, and for releasing venous blood from the legs. It is very good for developing tone in the tissues of an enlarged abdomen.

SUGGESTED SLANT BOARD EXERCISES

Follow the instructions carefully. You can feel relaxed, refreshed, and invigorated quickly by stimulating circulation to all parts of the body. Do not try to do too much at first. Take on more exercises gradually. Do not attempt exercises that might endanger your physical condition. If in doubt, have a physical checkup.

∽ Caution

Do not attempt to use the slant board until or unless you are able to get up and down easily from the floor. Those with heart con- ditions, high blood pressure, internal bleeding, or other serious health conditions, as well as pregnant women, should consult their doctors before using the slant board. Wait at least two hours after eating to use the board.

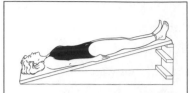

1. Lie flat on your back, allowing gravity to help shift abdominal organs into their proper positions and letting blood circulate to the head. Lie on board at least 10 minutes. This basic position should begin and end all series of exercises.

2. While lying on your back, stretch the abdomen by raising arms above head. Next, lower arms to sides. Raise and lower arms 10 to 15 times. This stretches the abdominal muscles and pulls the abdomen down toward the shoulders.

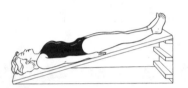

3. *If you are in great shape and under age forty, you may be able to proceed safely with the following exercise. Otherwise, wait until you have exercised for at least two weeks, then proceed carefully, taking care to avoid excessive abdominal strain. Consult your doctor if you are uncertain.* Take a deep breath and hold it. Still holding your breath, alternately flex (contract) and relax abdominal muscles 5 times. You should feel your abdomen pressing upward toward your shoulders as you flex and feel it dropping down a little as you relax. Take a normal breath, then repeat the exercise 10 to 15 times, breathing normally between sets.

4. Pat abdomen vigorously with open hands. Lean to one side and then to the other, patting 10 to 15 times on each side. Reverse sides 3 or 4 times. Next, bring the body to a sitting position, using the abdominal muscles. Return to lying position.

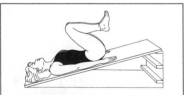

5. Holding onto the board, bring knees up toward chest. While in this position, (a) turn head from side to side 5 or 6 times, then (b) lift head slightly and rotate in circles 3 or 4 times. Reverse rotation. Repeat each set 2 or 3 times.

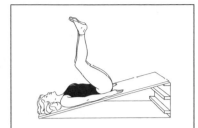

6. Holding onto the board, lift legs to a vertical position. Rotate legs outward in opposite circles 8 to 10 times. Change directions, rotating circles inward. Increase to 25 times after a week or two of exercising.

7. Raise legs to a vertical position. Keeping knees straight, slowly lower left leg to the board, then right leg. Raise each leg then lower each leg 15 to 25 times. Next, with legs in a vertical position, slowly lower both together to the board. Repeat 3 or 4 times.

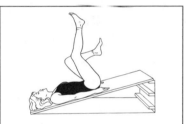

8. Raise legs to a vertical position. Bicycle legs in air 15 to 25 times. Do this at a slow pace at first, increasing speed gradually through the first week or two of regular exercise.

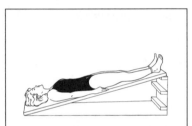

9. Lying flat on your back, relax completely, letting the blood circulate. Hold this position 5 to 15 minutes.

THREE SHAPING AND FIRMING EXERCISES FOR WOMEN

We find that some people profit more by a variety of exercises while others do better with only a few simple ones. The following exercises, if faithfully used, will do more to firm up and tone the body than most exercise programs. Reducing the calorie intake of foods lowers the weight, while correct exercise restores the right firmness and proportion to the body.

These exercises should be done first thing in the morning, after drinking a glass of water with a teaspoon of liquid chlorophyll. Wear pajamas, a sweatsuit, or an exercise outfit of some kind. It is best to keep up the exercises for three months at least.

Arm and Leg Shape-Up Exercise

Objective: For firming the arms from shoulders to wrists, and the upper legs, calves, and ankles.

Sit in a straight-backed chair, preferably one without arms. Cross your right leg over your left at the knee; bring up the right foot until the knee is almost straight. Extend both arms out straight in front of you and make tight fists. As you rotate your right foot from the ankle in circles to the right, rotate the right fist in a circle to the right and the left fist in a circle to the left. Keep the weight of the right leg resting on the left knee, but keep that foot up. The foot rotations may seem awkward but keep doing them. You'll get better at it.

After ten repetitions, reverse the direction of rotation of the right foot and the two arms and do ten more. Then, place the left leg over the right knee and repeat the whole process. Increase repetitions by five each month (in each direction with each foot).

Body Firm-Up Exercise

Objective: For firming the stomach, strengthening the abdominal muscles, firming the neck, shoulders, and arms, straightening the spine, eliminating swayback, and lifting the breasts.

Lie on your back on the floor. (For all floor exercises, lie on a thick rug or use an exercise mat.) Raise your knees and bring your feet back toward your buttocks as far as you can without discomfort, keeping your feet flat on the floor. With your elbows hugging your sides, touch each hand to the shoulder on its side, right hand to right shoulder, left hand to left shoulder. Now sweep your hands in a circular motion, out and up along the floor, until both hands come together above the head. At the same time you raise the arms, straighten out the legs. When you've reached the endpoint, stretch your hands up a little higher, and your feet down a little farther, so that you feel the muscles stretching throughout your body.

Return your arms and legs to the original position, then repeat ten times each day for the first week. Add two repetitions per week until you're up to thirty.

Changing the Bottom Line Exercise

Objective: Designed to take inches off the derriere and make lovely curves to replace the bulges. Now, this is not so much an exercise as a principle of exercise for this part of the body, and there are several different ways we can do it.

The first variation is called "the walk." Sit on the floor, legs outstretched in front of you, feet together, arms at your sides, elbows bent as if you were about to start a race. Twist your body

somewhat sharply to the left, then to the right, "walking" the but-tocks forward as you twist the torso and arms right—left—right—left, and so on. Keep it up for two minutes the first week, and extend to five minutes (or more) in three months.

The second variation, modeled on the first, involves the same movements, only remain in place and simply rock from side to side, not moving forward.

The third variation, another rocker, calls for sitting on the floor in the same position, extending your arms out sideways like airplane wings but keeping the elbows bent. Wag one "wing" at a time as you rock from one side to the other.

Since the second and third variations are easier, try to keep them up for five minutes if you opt to do them instead of the first, and increase the time you take doing them each week.

This is basically a three-month regimen, but it may take less time for some and more for others to firm up the body.

SYSTEM FOR IMPROVING THE REAR VIEW (AND THIGHS)

The thighs and rear are the most difficult for many women to keep as slender and toned as they would like. But here are some exercises especially designed for a two-month program to get the flab off the buttocks and upper thighs.

Some physical fitness experts say that spot reducing is impossible because any exercise uses up calories, which are more or less uniformly taken from all over the body, but I have seen too many examples of successful spot reducing to believe that. I feel that the caloric demand takes place in the tissue being exercised, and that localized fatty deposits are removed first.

Many times we find that an enlarged "rear view" is associated with lower back problems, so we have to take care of this part of the anatomy as we do the rest of the body. A tendency to gain weight in the lower half of the body but not the upper half (or vice versa) can be due to a pituitary imbalance, and some women patients report that the Chinese herb Dong quai has helped them with this problem, while ginseng has helped men. The herbs must be used along with exercise for best results, to help balance the body proportions.

Hip Roll

Lie flat on your back, arms at your sides, palms on the floor, legs out straight; then draw up your left knee toward your chest. Keeping your upper torso flat against the floor and leaving your right leg straight, twist your hips to the right until your left knee touches the floor. Repeat ten times and do the same thing with your right leg and knee. (See knee crossover, hip roll figure on page 95.)

Hip Roll (Variation)

When you can do the first exercise easily, try bringing up both knees and doing the same thing—roll your hips and swing your knees to the right, not touching the floor, then to the left, starting with ten repetitions. The exercise is slightly easier if you turn your head in the opposite direction as you are swing-ing your knees. Work up to twenty-five of these in two months by adding two repetitions each week.

Straight Kicks, Lying Down

Lie on your back with your arms at your sides, your right knee up, right foot flat on the floor, and your left leg straight. Smoothly kick your right leg straight up (as high as you can). Repeat ten times. Then do the same with the left leg, ten times. Work up to thirty in two months.

Flipper-Flaps

Lie on one side and support your upper torso in an upright position, while bending the underneath knee into an "L" shape. Now begin lifting the top leg—up, down, up, down. Start with six, and work up to eighteen on each side. Vary by keeping the top leg bent during the lifts. (See side leg lifts fig-ure on page 97.)

Swim Kick

Lying on your stomach, support your upper torso partly on your forearms and look straight ahead, raising your feet about a foot off the floor. Tighten your buttocks and kick as though swimming, twenty repetitions each leg, working your way up to three minutes of rapid kicking at each session in two months.

Leg Lifts, Reverse

Lying on your stomach, arms at sides, palms face up on the floor. Turn your head to your most comfortable side, and separate your feet 6 inches. Take a deep breath. Lift the right leg, point the toe, contract the buttocks, count to three, let out the breath, lower the leg, and relax the buttocks. Keep your pelvis flat on the floor throughout the exercise. Switch to the left leg and do the same to the count of three, exhaling as you lower your leg and relax your buttocks. Start with six on each leg; increase three each week to thirty repetitions. (See more leg lifts figure on page 97.)

Pony Kick

Get down on all fours, with your hands far enough apart for comfortable support, and knees about a foot apart. Extend your left leg behind you, off the floor, knee slightly bent. Now lift and lower

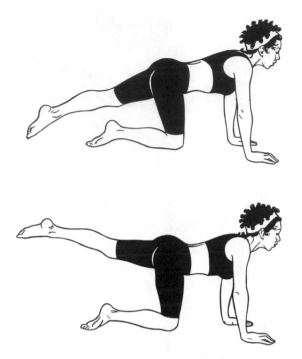

your leg, smoothly but rapidly, ten times. Then repeat with the other leg ten times. Build up to thirty repetitions in two months.

Erect Kick

Standing up straight, feet together, kick as high forward as you can with your right leg, ten times. Repeat with the left leg. Don't jerk or use too much strength the first week. Add five kicks each week, and aim for kicking above your head.

Teetering

This one is fun. Get on your knees, spine erect, palms on thighs. Holding your head and body straight, tense your buttocks, inhale deeply, and lean back as far as you can hold without straining. Hold to a slow count of five. Breathe out and go back to a relaxed upright position. Do five and try to build up to twenty repetitions in two months.

Arch Lift

Lie on your back on the floor, arms at sides, palms down; lift your knees and bring both feet back until they are flat on the floor. Take a deep breath as you raise your buttocks, arching your pelvis and lower back off the floor. Go only as far as you can without straining, and hold to the slow count of five before slowly coming back down. Do four of these the first week, working up to ten repetitions in two months. Try to get a little farther off the floor after the second week, and as you improve, increase the count to seven, then nine, then eleven, and so on.

Cool Down

Finish with ten minutes of bouncing on a mini-trampoline, calisthenics, or dance movements to fast music with a good beat.

Different people progress at different rates. If you like these exercises but are not quite sure where you want to be in two months, keep them up.

OTHER WAYS TO STAY FIT

There are many types of exercises and many ways to get exercise, such as gardening, weeding, washing windows, mowing the lawn, washing the car, taking the stairs instead of the elevator, or riding a bicycle to a nearby market to get a few things instead of taking the car. Think about it. Most of us drive too much. Legs were made to walk with, and we can all benefit from as much walking as possible.

Our legs are the pumps that drive the venous blood back to the heart, and using them often is the key to good circulation and cardiovascular health. Blood tends to stagnate in the leg veins if we don't get enough exercise, and this may lead to varicose veins. Dr. Paul Dudley White, the late President Eisenhower's heart specialist, often pointed out that we die from our feet up. He once said that if you have flabby legs, you will have a flabby brain—a lighthearted comment, but one with more than a grain of truth in it. There is considerable evidence to indicate that firm, well-exercised legs lead to a long life, and this is what I saw in the Hunza Valley of Pakistan where men over one hundred years old walked up and down mountain paths each day to work in the fields on the terraced hillsides.

Check out the nature trails closest to where you live and visit them with a friend or two. Make sure they are safe, and use them as often as you can. If you live by a beach, lake, or forest, walk where your eyes can feast on beauty. Beautiful sights are the vitamins and minerals of the mind.

Fresh air and sunshine are vital elements of health, too, and one way to get more of them is to go bicycling or hiking in the country. Backpacking and jogging are wonderful forms of exercise, but are strenuous unless you are in shape. Horseback riding exercises most of the muscles of the body. Camping is a light exercise form of recreation, but plan meals carefully in advance. It is all too easy to build up a great appetite and overeat.

The better the physical condition we are in, the more efficiently the body works, and the trimmer we stay— as long as we remain aware and in control of what goes into the mouth.

NURTURING OF THE SKIN AND CARE OF WRINKLES

Wrinkles in the skin have many causes—poor diet, lack of certain vitamins and minerals, dryness due to exposure to sun and wind, flabby muscle structure beneath the skin, and habitual patterns of facial expression. For example, frowning is said to involve a pattern of facial muscle stretching that encourages a particularly unattractive wrinkle pattern over the years. Another cause of wrinkles is loss of subcutaneous fat due to weight reduction. These wrinkles tend to go away as new skin replaces the old, but we can do much to hasten the process.

We find that a healthy diet sometimes brings on elimination through the skin—unsightly blemishes and various types of eruptions as the body is being cleansed of old toxic wastes and catarrh. Worry and anxiety are also believed to contribute to skin troubles. Once the cleansing is over, the skin troubles will vanish and the skin will be softer and more beautiful than ever.

The skin is basically a silicon organ, and foods richest in silicon, such as alfalfa sprouts and rice polishings, will enhance its texture. The skin needs vitamin A especially, but also B-complex and vitamins E and F.

Iodine foods are needed, and one of the foods highest in iodine is Nova Scotia dulse, a member of the seaweed family. The Japanese eat over seventy varieties of seaweed because it is rich in minerals, including trace minerals needed in very

CHEMICAL CONTENTS OF KELP	
Iodine	0.18 percent
Calcium	1.05 percent
Phosphorus	0.34 percent
Iron	0.37 percent
Copper	0.0008 percent
Potassium	11.15 percent
Magnesium	0.74 percent
Sodium	3.98 percent
Chlorine	13.07 percent
Manganese	0.0015 percent
Sulfur	1.0 percent

small amounts by the body. A chemical analysis of a sample of kelp showed the following mineral contents, all vital to health.

Skin brushing with a natural bristle brush not only hastens skin elimination, removes dead skin cells, and stimulates elasticity and tone in the underlying new skin structure, but it also helps get rid of cellulite, the layer of subcutaneous fat that tends to pucker the skin on overweight or physically inactive women.

Regular forms of exercise will tone the muscle tissue underlying the skin and improve blood circulation to the skin areas, but there are several exercises that are especially helpful in reducing or eliminating facial wrinkles.

FACIAL EXERCISE SYSTEM
FOR SKIN TONING

It is best to do these exercises ten times, three times each day, but it is also good to practice them in odd moments during the day. Either make sure no one is around or tell people what you're doing so they won't think you're strange.

Wrinkles Under the Eyes

First, look straight ahead, then, keeping the head in that position, look up at the sky or ceiling and wink five times, rest, wink five times more, and so on. This will help get rid of wrinkles in the lower eyelids. In the usual way of winking, only the upper eyelids get the exercise.

Crow's Feet

Crow's feet at the corners of the eyes can be helped by raising and lowering the eyebrows, which also exercises forehead muscles. Also, rolling the fingertips over the wrinkled area behind the eyes (sides of forehead), twice a day will help. Any time you can bring cold water to the facial wrinkles, you will help tone the muscles underneath them.

Temple and Forehead Muscles

These muscles are also strengthened by squeezing the eyes tightly shut. Many times an inverted cold spoon on the eye will help wrinkles disappear. Do this many times a day.

Cheeks and Muscles Around the Mouth

There are several wonderful exercises to tone the cheeks and muscles around the mouth. One is to pucker the lips, then stretch the corners of the mouth wide, as in grinning. Another is to pucker the lips, then move them alternately to the left and to the right. A third is to open the mouth wide, hold it open, and move the lips. A fourth is to lift the cheek muscles, as in squinting the eyes, then relax them.

Chin Wrinkles

Chin wrinkles are helped by raising the lower lip above the upper lip and bringing it back to normal position.

Throat Wrinkles

To help smooth throat wrinkles, tilt the head back as far as possible, then pucker the lips and wrinkle up your nose at the same time.

The Honey Pat

This is another special technique for getting rid of wrinkles and helping remove blackheads and whiteheads from the skin. Pour a little honey in a saucer, dip your fingers in it, and apply it to the face, drawing the facial skin and muscles out with the sticky honey. This exercises the muscles and pores and helps develop the tone of the underlying tissue. Do this ten times daily for two months, together with skin brushing exercises.

In general, I do not believe in using lotions, creams, and salves, but I feel that apricot kernel oil is very soothing to the skin.

Keep in mind that skin cells are replaced very rapidly and the smoothing of wrinkles from loss of fatty tissue will not take long, especially if aided by the preceding exercises.

A FINAL NOTE OF ADVICE ON EXERCISE

There are many kinds of exercise, and all have their special benefits. Pick the system that will help tone the part of your body that needs it the most, and stay with it until you feel you are ready to move on with another system.

CHAPTER 6

MY HEALTH AND HARMONY FOOD REGIMEN

Sooner or later, we have to get away from diets and turn to a right way of eating, a right way of living. I don't even like the word "diet." It conjures up thoughts of hospitals and doctors and nutritionists with special meal plans tailored for people who are seriously ill. When we stop and think about it, a diet is sometimes a deliberately imbalanced eating regimen designed to counter an imbalanced health condition. But it can also be imbalanced through ignorance or carelessness.

Here I am teaching a balanced way of living, and we find out that if we have a balanced way of living, we don't have to cut back on the food we should have. A good food regimen isn't a matter of always eating the foods we like, since there are many foods that are good for us and we can learn to like them. For instance, I didn't like avocados to begin with, but I like them now. A lot of people don't like okra, but it is a wonderful food. So is asparagus. We should learn to appreciate and take greater pleasure in a much wider variety of foods than we have been accustomed to.

I was on a weight-gaining diet once—four milkshakes a day with whipped cream and a cherry on top—and I almost died from it. Any limited and often repeated food regimen is technically a diet. There are coffee and donut diets, meat and potato diets, hamburger and French fry diets, juice diets, cabbage and peanut diets—all kinds of diets—and they are killing the people who eat them. So it makes a great deal of sense to get off diets, to get away from imbalanced food habits.

As I have said before, weight loss and weight management are like learning to play the piano. You have to practice, practice, practice to do it well. In the learning stages you will make mistakes, but never mind—keep practicing. The skill you gain in practicing, with constant application, will become beautiful music. Practice makes perfect, as they say. The day will come when playing will not require such concentration and effort because it will be natural to you. With perseverance, the "new you" will emerge as surely as the sun rises in the morning.

WHAT YOU DON'T KNOW CAN HURT

Most Americans develop food preferences during childhood, from the patterns of food, cooking, and preparation used in the parents' home. Teenage girls may learn a little more about cooking and nutrition in high school, but since it isn't a "real-life" situation, such facts are often quickly forgotten. Newly married wives try to discover the sorts of things their husbands like to eat, then incorporate these into the menu plans of their new home lives. When we stop and think about it, most food decisions made at the supermarket and in the kitchen are not centered around nutritional value, but around cost, taste, convenience, ease of cooking, advertising, hearsay, and tradition.

The first thing I want to tell you is that the average American eats far too much milk and wheat. A government survey showed that 56 percent of the American diet is made up of these two products—40 percent dairy products and 16 percent wheat products. Both are fattening, especially in those quantities. I believe that the pasteurization of milk and the refining of wheat into flour alter these foods in such a way that they are more fattening and more difficult for the body to handle than in their natural, whole state. Wheat is one of the most fattening of the grains. People who eat this much wheat and milk are wheat logged and milk logged. Allergy doctors will tell you this is a high catarrh–producing diet, and allergies often develop after this high amount of catarrh. We find that catarrh is associated with practically all allergy conditions, bronchitis, coughs, colds, flu, pneumonia, hay fever, asthma, and so forth.

Milk and wheat should not total more than 6 percent of all the foods taken in. If we could get them down to 6 percent, we would balance our diets and stay away from many of our weight problems. My Health and Harmony Food Regimen will take care of most health problems.

When the kitchen is ruled by ignorance, the dining room table leads to the doctor's office and to the doctor bills that naturally follow.

As we look at how we are living in the United States, especially over the last thirty years, we see that diet and trends in buying foods as related to the way foods are advertised may be the reason why over 50 percent of the people are overweight. The three foods advertised most are wheat, milk, and sugar.

The amount of these three foods in the average diet violates the Law of Excess; for example, the American diet consists of 16 percent wheat products, 40 percent milk-containing dairy products, and at least 11 percent sugar. If we add up these percentages, the total is 67 percent. I wonder if we are squeezing out the very foods that would keep us at a normal weight. Wheat, milk, and sugar are fat-forming foods, and because they are overused, I am sure they are contributing to the ill health and overweight problem in America. We have had patients who cut out only these three foods and used substitutes instead, resulting in a considerable loss of excess pounds. In nearly all cases where people have stopped using these three foods in excess, we have found very good results in overweight cases. I believe that 67 percent is too much, and these foods should run only about 10 percent of our total diets. This is especially necessary when we are trying to get well.

The cure for ignorance is knowledge, and I think it is wonderful that nature is so generous and willing to point us in the right direction. My Health and Harmony Food Regimen is taken from nature's kitchen. You and your family can live well and be healthy following it.

CLEANING OUT THE CUPBOARDS AND PANTRY

If we want to clean out the body, we can go on an elimination diet. But if we want to keep it clean, we have to clean out the cupboards and pantry. We have to stop eating the wrong foods before eating the right foods will do us much good.

The first things to get rid of are white flour and white sugar—the refined carbohydrates. These are hard on the pancreas, adrenals, liver, kidneys, and bowel, and are probably even more responsible for obesity than high-fat foods. We must have fiber in our foods from the complex carbohydrates, fresh fruits and vegetables, whole grains, and so on. Instead of sugar, use a little honey now and then for sweetening, or use naturally sweet fruits and dried fruits, such as figs, dates, raisins, dried apricots, and so forth.

It is better to use herb seasonings than spices, and you will be surprised at the delightful flavors you can get with herbs. Use cayenne pepper instead of black pepper, which is hard on the liver. Cayenne pepper is good for the digestion and circulation.

Cut back on the use of dairy products, since many Americans are milk logged, which can be catarrh producing, constipating, and definitely fattening. Yogurt and kefir are better for those over age forty who have a hard time digesting milk products, and they are best when they are raw. Clabbered milk is also easily digestible. Soy milk, rice milk, and the raw nut and seed milks offer wonderful alternatives.

I feel that it is to your advantage to eliminate all fatty meats from the diet. Cut back on the use of red meat and substitute more fish and poultry instead. Fish should have fins, scales, and white meat. Salmon is also very good. Meat should be baked or broiled, never fried. Don't use meat fat (such as bacon grease or lard) for any cooking purpose.

Avoid coffee, tea, and all soft drinks. Caffeine is hard on the nerves, sugar is a nutritional disaster, and artificial sweeteners are considered harmful by many scientists. For example, saccharine, a coal-tar derivative, has been linked to cancer. Herb teas and natural coffee substitutes are much better for you. Use decaffeinated coffee if you must; but it still has 2 percent caffeine, and the same coffee acids develop when it sits in the pot.

Since my regimen includes many fresh fruits and vegetables, you will be getting more water from them and you won't need to drink as much liquid with or between meals as on your former food regimen.

You may be using food items I have not listed here that are valueless or harmful. Read the label, think about the product, and ask questions. You should evaluate what you intend to put into your body. Use whole grain flours for baking, but try to cut down on baked goods and on the use of wheat products in general. Most Americans eat far too much wheat, and a wheat-logged body can become imbalanced to the point of being susceptible to allergies and obesity.

Throw out the table salt, and do not buy salt substitutes unless they are natural. Salt has been linked to hypertension and water retention. There are vegetable seasonings, broth powders, and herbs that make lovely flavor enhancers for vegetables and proteins. They are good for us, without harmful side effects, and some taste "salty."

Iceberg lettuce has so little food value that leaf lettuce is by far the better buy. Why waste the money? Most citrus is picked green for shipping, so I recommend against it. If you can get tree-ripened citrus, it is all right to eat it, sliced in sections, for the bulk value. There are many other fruits in season for you to eat, and you should have a variety. Fresh, sun-ripened fruits are best.

Throw out most packaged and canned products, and anything else that has been processed or contains chemical additives. Processing reduces food value and increases price, and you are paying for labor—not increased worth. Most canned and packaged foods contain salt, sugar, or both, in addition to chemical preservatives, colorings, flavor enhancers, texturizers, moisturizers, and various other chemicals. These are unnatural to the body, and untold harm may result from them over the long term. Packaging, canning, and chemicals add to the cost of the food as well. Additives react most strongly with the fat cells, where drugs and toxic materials are stored. I am opposed to using hybrid foods and genetically engineered foods simply because I believe that food sources that depart from nature are never really safe to eat. I advise only whole, pure, natural, and fresh foods for those who are serious about living a healthy life.

FOOD LAWS TO FOLLOW

Nature has given us bodies that respond best to foods in certain combinations and amounts, as listed below. A rule of thumb for eating is to never eat until you have a keen desire for simple food. Don't eat if you are ill, emotionally upset, or feel chilled. Eat only small portions of easily digested foods if you are tired or fatigued.

The family should eat at the same table at the same time, keeping conversation pleasant. The table is no place for discipline, scolding, insults, or verbal abuse of any kind. Food should be adequately chewed—especially raw vegetables and starches. One way to discourage eating too rapidly is to put the fork down between bites. Teach your children that it is always healthier to eat too little than too much.

1. Daily Diet

Daily diet should be 80 percent alkaline and 20 percent acid foods, as shown in Table 6.1 on page 123. This means that you should select eight alkaline foods and two acid foods daily.

2. Natural

Fifty percent to 60 percent of the food eaten should be raw. If, for any reason, you can't follow this law, take 1 teaspoon of wheat bran or psyllium husks after each meal. This will take care of the fiber needed in your diet.

3. Proportion

Eat six vegetables, two fruits, one starch, and one protein daily. (This keeps your daily food total 80 percent alkaline, 20 percent acid.) This matches what the blood should be.

4. Variety

Vary proteins, starches, vegetables, and fruits from meal to meal and day to day. Know seven good proteins, seven good starches, seven good salad dressings, seven herb teas—to get a variety.

5. Excess

Excess in one or a few foods is to be avoided because this creates imbalance in the body. Wheat, milk, and sugar are the greatest offenders I know, and they all contribute to weight problems. Excess eating of all foods, even in a balanced eating regimen, leads to the development of fatty tissue, a condition of imbalance within the body. Any form of excess leads to imbalance of some kind.

6. Deficiency

Deficiency in foods containing the chemical elements, vitamins, and other nutrients causes imbalance in the body and, in general, prevents tissue repair and rebuilding. This is especially important with regard to inherently weak organs of the body, which are unable to hold nutrients and chemical elements as well as normal tissues. The most common deficiencies I have encountered are calcium, sodium, silicon, and iodine, and these should be obtained from foods or supplements derived from foods.

7. Combinations

Separate proteins and starches: one at lunch, one at dinner. Have fruit for breakfast and, if desired, at 3 P.M. If reducing, have two protein meals and only one starch meal in the regular regimen.

Table 6.1. **Acid–Alkaline Food**

Nonstarch Foods

AL	Alfalfa	AL	Celery knobs
AL	Artichokes	AL	Chicory
AL	Asparagus	AL	Coconut
AL	Beans (string)	AL	Corn
AL	Beans (wax)	AL	Cucumbers
AL	Beet leaves	AL	Dandelions
AL	Beets (whole)	AL	Eggplant
AL	Broccoli	AL	Endive
AL	Cabbage (red)	AL	Garlic
AL	Cabbage (white)	AL	Horseradish
AL	Carrot tops	AL	Kale
AL	Carrots	AL	Kohlrabi
AL	Cauliflower	AL	Leeks

(Continued)

Table 6.1. **Continued**

Nonstarch Foods

AL	Lettuce	AL	Rutabagas
AL	Mushrooms	AL	Savory
AL	Okra	AL	Sea lettuce
AL	Olives (ripe)	AL	Sorrel
AL	Onions	AL	Soybean (products)
AL	Osterplant	AL	Spinach
AL	Parsley	AL	Sprouts
AL	Parsnips	AL	Summer squash
AL	Peas (fresh)	AL	Swiss chard
AL	Peppers (sweet)	AL	Turnips
AL	Radishes	AL	Watercress

Proteins and Fruits

AL	Apples	AC	Fish
AL	Apricots	AC	Goose
AL	Avocados	AL	Grapes
AC	Beef	AL	Honey (pure)
AL	Berries (all)	AC	Jell-O
AC	Buttermilk	AC	Lamb
AL	Cantaloupes	AL	Lemons
AC	Chicken	AL	Limes
AC	Clams	AC	Lobster
AC	Cottage cheese	AC	Mutton
AC	Crab	AC	Nuts
AL	Cranberries	AL	Oranges
AL	Currants	AC	Oyster
AL	Dates	AL	Peaches
AC	Duck	AL	Pears
AC	Eggs	AL	Persimmons
AL	Figs	AL	Pineapple

AL Plums	AL Rhubarb
AC Pork	AL Tomatoes
AL Prunes	AC Turkey
AC Rabbit	AC Turtle
AL Raisins	AC Veal
AC Raw sugar	

Starchy Foods

AL Bananas	AC Millet rye
AC Barley	AC Oatmeal
AC Beans (lima)	AC Peanut butter
AC Beans (white)	AC Peanuts
AC Bread	AC Peas (dried)
AC Cereals	AC Potatoes (sweet)
AC Chestnuts	AL Potatoes (white)
AC Corn	AL Pumpkin
AC Cornmeal	AC Rice (brown)
AC Cornstarch	AC Rice (polished)
AC Crackers	AC Rye flour
AC Gluten flour	AC Sauerkraut
AC Grapefruit	AL Squash (hubbard)
AC Lentils	AC Tapioca
AC Macaroni	AC Whole wheat
AC Maize	

Source: Ragnar Berg of Germany.

Note: Foods preceded by the letters *AL* are alkaline forming; foods preceded by the letters *AC* are acid forming.

8. Cooking

Cook with low heat, without water, or with only a little water in waterless cookware, lid left on. Don't peek; leave the lid on until done to avoid air exposure to hot food. Waterless cooking at 185°F destroys only 2 percent of nutrients, as compared to 20 percent in steaming (212°F) and 50 percent in boiling foods. Use unsprayed vegetables, if available, and prepare them as soon after picking as possible. Steaming, of course, is preferable to boiling.

9. Bake, Broil, or Roast

If meat is used, choose lean meat—no fat, no pork. Never fry or cook in heated oils.

It is important for us to realize that we should take more of our foods on the raw side, which is not as fattening and has the advantage of providing more live enzymes to help the body use its nutrients better. Raw vegetables in a salad are wonderful for us. We can even use raw asparagus, squash, and spinach in salads.

We can put raw foods in a liquifier and have blended fruit or vegetable drinks. I call them health cocktails. Of course, we must be careful about adding cream or butter.

Most people eat too many acid-forming foods: meat, eggs, milk, wheat products, and starchy foods. As we have mentioned, a government survey has shown that 54 percent of the average American diet is made up of wheat and milk products. These are the greatest weight builders when taken in excess. These foods should only be 6 percent of the American diet. We need to eat more fresh vegetables and fruits with our meals. In doing this, we reduce taking in too many starches and proteins, and we produce a better acid/alkaline balance.

Vegetables and fruits not only provide a vital source of vitamins and minerals, and a steady supply of glucose easily handled by the bloodstream, but they provide much-needed fiber for colon health. A recent national diet survey showed that the average American fiber intake is low, about 7 grams of fiber per 1,000 calories. This is far from sufficient. A survey commissioned by the Archway Company showed that 76 percent of the adults surveyed knew that fiber was important in their nutrition intake but 99 percent didn't have any idea how much soluble fiber to consume each day and only 55 percent could name foods that are good sources of fiber. Fiber is found in whole grain cereals, breads, and fruits and vegetables. Supplements of wheat bran or oat bran, very high in fiber, can be added to soups, salads, and breakfast cereals. People who eat mostly whole, pure, and natural foods get enough fiber daily from their diets. According to a 1996 study published in the *Journal of the American Medical Association,* each 10-gram increase in daily fiber intake reduces the risk of heart attack by 30 percent. The American Dietetic Association recommends 20 to 25 grams of fiber daily.

The following instructions were given to the cooks at our sanitarium to carry out our idea of natural, whole, and pure. These are not reducing ideas but a maintenance diet for the average person. Most people will not gain weight on this diet. There are many lovely ideas here for those who want to get into food planning in the future.

Upon arising, drink a glass of warm water—add a teaspoon of liquid chlorophyll, if desired. This is especially effective as an aid to good bowel function.

A half hour before breakfast, take unsweetened fruit juice such as grape, pineapple, prune, fig, apple, or black cherry juice. Liquid chlorophyll in water or a broth or lecithin drink may be taken instead. Add 1 tablespoon vegetable broth powder and/or 1 tablespoon lecithin granules to a glass of warm water. Herbal teas are also recommended.

Between juice or drink and breakfast, I suggest that you skin brush for two to five minutes, exercise on a bouncer to music, take a walk in a garden or a short hike, or do other exercise.

BREAKFAST

Have fresh fruit, a health drink, and one starch; or two fruits, one protein, and a health drink; or fruit only. In boiling water, soak dried fruits such as unsulfured apricots, prunes, figs, apples, or pears for five minutes before using. Fresh fruit of any kind may be used—melons, grapes, peaches, pears, berries, or apples. Use fruit in season when possible; don't eat melons and sour fruit together. Sprinkle baked or stewed fruit with ground nuts or nut butter, especially sesame nut butter.

The following menus are adapted from instructions to the kitchen staff members when my sanitarium at the Ranch was in full swing.

Fruit

One fresh fruit and one dried fruit. For reducing, cut down on dried fruits. Prunes have a lot of fiber.

Drinks

Raw nut or seed milk, soy milk, or rice milk, if desired; whey; and tea (three different kinds of teas should be served during the day; five different kinds should be kept on hand in the kitchen).

Cereals

Always serve five different kinds during the week: Yellow cornmeal (twice a week), muesli (twice a week), rye, brown rice, and millet. Whole grain cereal should be cooked over very low heat, tightly covered; use a double boiler or soak overnight in boiling water in a wide-mouth thermos.

Supplements

For sprinkling on cereals or fruits: Wheat germ, rice polishings, flaxseed meal, and sesame seed meal.

Eggs

Soft and hard boiled or poached.

Sunday Mornings

Okay to serve cornmeal hot cakes with honey or pure maple syrup.

Coffee Substitutes

Any of the toasted grain or vegetable-based products.

10 A.M.

Juice time—vegetable or fruit; or substitute vegetable broth.

SUGGESTED BREAKFAST MENUS

Monday
Fresh fruit

Reconstituted dried apricots

Millet

Supplements

Oatstraw tea

(Add eggs or cottage cheese for protein)

Tuesday
Fresh figs

Cornmeal cereal

Supplements

Shavegrass tea

(Add eggs or nut butter, if desired,

or raw applesauce and blackberries)

or coddled egg, supplements, and herb tea

Wednesday
Fresh fruit

Reconstituted dried peaches

Millet cereal

Supplements

Add eggs or cheese for protein

Alfalfa tea

Thursday
Fresh fruit

Reconstituted prunes

Brown rice (cold or warm) with

raisins, cinnamon, sunflower seeds, honey

For protein, yogurt with fruit and nut butter

Supplements

Herb tea

Friday
Slices of fresh pineapple with shredded coconut
Buckwheat cereal
Supplements
Peppermint tea
or baked apple, persimmons, chopped raw almonds,
Acidophilus milk, supplements, and herb tea

Saturday
Muesli with bananas, dates, and seed, nut, or rice milk
Supplements
Dandelion coffee or herb tea

Sunday
Cooked applesauce with raisins
Rye cereal
Supplements
Shavegrass tea
or cantaloupe and strawberries, cottage cheese,
supplements, and herb tea

When starting out with a new diet or eating regimen, it is best for the cook to allow the family a transition time to get used to the changes. Rushing people or trying to force them breeds counterproductive results. So, be patient.

The basics of this daily food regimen are two different fruits, six or more vegetables, one protein, and one starch, using fruit or vegetable juices or herb teas as between-meal snacks. Chlorophyll tea (1 teaspoon liquid chlorophyll in 1 cup of hot water) can be used in place of fruit juice. Use at least two green leafy vegetables every day. I advise that 50 to 60 percent of the total intake be raw food. Isn't that easy to remember?

LUNCH

Salad Bar

Always serve: Finely shredded carrots, beets, turnips, carrot sticks, celery sticks, sliced tomatoes, sliced cucumbers, sliced green peppers, alfalfa sprouts (other sprouts served occasionally).

Anything else in season, used raw: Jicama, zucchini, summer squash, onions (small), parsley, watercress, endive.

Twice a week: Stuffed celery (almond or cashew butter).

Once or twice a week: Olives, Waldorf salad (peel apples), gelatin mold (with shredded carrots and pineapple).

Once a week: Carrot and pea salad with cheese, cole slaw, carrot and cashew salad (made with Champion juicer), stuffed dates (almond or cashew butter).

Salad dressings: Using mashed avocado, yogurt, or nut butter as a base; add cottage cheese, blue cheese, Romano cheese, or Parmesan cheese together with your favorite herbal seasonings. Traditional oil and vinegar with a little honey is always acceptable. Use as little dressing as possible—a tablespoon or two—to avoid excess calories.

Vegetables

Two cooked. Use one grown under the ground and one grown above the ground. One bland vegetable must be served, such as beets, squash (yellow neck, banana, winter, etc.), zucchini, peas, carrots, string beans, wax beans, spinach, or asparagus. Other vegetables may include a sulphur type, such as cabbage, cauliflower, brussels sprouts, onions, broccoli, turnips, or kohlrabi. Steamed onions may be served (creamed with parsley) once a week, as a separate dish.

Starches

Brown rice (twice a week), baked potato (twice a week), lima beans, cornbread, yams.

Drinks

Milk, whey, buttermilk, nut milk drink (once a week), herb tea, coffee substitute.

SUGGESTED LUNCH MENUS

Monday
Vegetable salad
Baby lima beans
Baked potato
Spearmint tea

Tuesday
Vegetable salad with health mayonnaise
Steamed asparagus
Very ripe bananas
or steamed unpolished brown rice
Vegetable broth or herb tea

Wednesday
Raw salad plate with sour cream dressing
Cooked green beans
Cornbread and/or baked hubbard squash
Sassafras tea

Thursday

Salad with French dressing

Baked zucchini and okra

Corn on the cob

Ry-Krisp

Buttermilk or herb tea

Friday

Salad

Baked green peppers stuffed with eggplant and tomatoes

Baked potato and/or bran muffin

Carrot soup or herb tea

Saturday

Salad

Turnips and turnip greens

Baked yam

Catnip tea

Sunday

Salad with lemon and olive oil dressing

Steamed whole barley

Cream of celery soup

Steamed chard

Herb tea

Four Best Starches and Others

The four best starches are yellow cornmeal, rye, brown rice, and millet. Other starches include barley (winter starch), buckwheat, baked or dead ripe banana, winter squash, baked potato, and baked sweet potato. For variety, include steel-cut oatmeal, whole wheat cereal, Shredded Wheat, rye crackers, bran muffins, bread (whole grain, rye, soy, cornbread, bran breads preferred).

Best Health Drinks

The best health drinks are vegetable broth, soup, coffee substitutes, buttermilk, raw milk, goat milk, rice milk, soy milk, raw nut or seed milk, oat straw tea, alfalfa-mint tea, huckleberry tea, mint tea, whey, carrot juice, V-8 juice, or any health drink. Water is often the most needed health drink, especially for the elderly.

Vegetarians

Use soybeans, lima beans, cottage cheese, sunflower seeds, and other seeds; also seed butters, nut butters, nut milk drinks, tofu, and eggs. Use meat substitutes or vegetarian proteins.

Twice a week: Low-fat cottage cheese or any cheese that breaks.

Once a week: Egg omelet. If you have a protein at this meal, health dessert is allowed but not recommended. Avoid eating proteins and starches together. They are deliberately separated on all meal plans so that you will eat more vegetables. The noon meal may be exchanged for the evening meal, provided the same regimen is upheld. Exercise is necessary to handle raw food; generally, more exercise is applied after the noon meal. Sandwiches, if eaten, should be combined with vegetables at the same meal.

DINNER

Protein

Meat (lean; no fat, no pork), such as chicken, turkey, meat loaf, lamb roast. A meat meal is to be served three times a week.

Fish

Have fish at least one day a week. Baked fish, such as ocean white fish, halibut, bass, trout, and salmon loaf, are good. Fresh salmon and canned sardines are very high in RNA (ribonucleic acid) for tissue rebuilding.

Vegetables

Have two cooked vegetables and salad, as for lunch.

Fruit and Cheese

Two nights a week, have three kinds of assorted fresh fruit, such as melons, apples, persimmons, pears, cherries, berries, oranges, apricots, peaches, or dates. Have assorted cheeses, such as Swiss, jack, cheddar, cottage cheese. Yogurt is also a good option. Crackers such as Ry-Krisp, Ak-Mak, or sesame can be included.

Juices

It is all right to have a juice in place of any meal. Those on juice diets should have juice every three hours as follows: 8 A.M.—fruit juice; 11 A.M.—carrot juice; 2 P.M.—carrot juice; 5 P.M.—fruit juice.

Vegetarians

Nut loaf is a good protein option for vegetarians. Cheese souf-flé, cottage cheese loaf, and eggplant and cheese loaf are great cheese options.

SUGGESTED DINNER MENUS

Monday

Salad

Diced celery and carrots

Steamed spinach (waterless cooked)

Puffy omelet

Vegetable broth

Tuesday

Salad

Cooked beet tops

Broiled steak or ground beef patties

Cauliflower

Comfrey tea

Wednesday

Cottage cheese

Cheese sticks

Apples, peaches, grapes, nuts

Apple concentrate cocktail

Thursday

Salad

Steamed chard

Baked eggplant

Grilled liver and onions

Persimmon whip (optional)

Alfa-mint tea

Friday

Salad with yogurt and lemon dressing

Steamed mixed greens

Beets

Steamed fish (with lemon slices)

Leek soup

Saturday

Salad

Cooked string beans

Baked summer squash

Carrot and cheese loaf

Cream of lentil soup or lemongrass tea

Fresh peach gelatin

Almond nut cream

Sunday

Salad

Diced carrots and peas

Steamed tomato aspic

Roast leg of lamb

Mint tea

MENU EXCHANGES

If the noon and evening meals are exchanged, follow the same regimen. Starches make you sleepy; proteins are stimulating. If insomnia is a problem, the meals may be switched for better results. Starch meals are for physical labor; proteins for mental work.

Never eat when emotionally upset, chilled, overtired, over-heated, ill, or lacking the keenest desire for the simplest food.

Missing a meal will do you more good than eating. Some may want to have an extra juice about 8:00 P.M.

Fruit juice may be apple, grape, papaya or liquid chlorophyll (½ to 1 teaspoon to an 8-ounce glass of water). Liquid chlorophyll may be used at 8 P.M. instead of juice. Those trying to lose weight can substitute a chlorophyll and water drink for any fruit or fruit juice.

Desserts: Always allowed on Sunday and two times a week. Gelatin mold (two times a week). Homemade ice cream (frozen fruit, whey, and honey). Carrot cake, custard, gelatin mold (cherry, grape, raspberry), apple betty, or yogurt with fresh fruit.

Avoid: All fried foods, foods cooked in hot oil, peanuts, peanut butter, sausage, salami, white flour products, sugar and sugar-rich foods, pickled foods, salted foods, table salt, dips, chocolate, and milk-containing products.

SUPPLEMENTS

Most people who have subsisted a number of years on poor diets find they are short of biochemical elements. They have lived on devitaminized, demineralized foodstuffs. For this reason, we recommend several supplements for rebuilding and revitalizing. They are not necessary to the person who has been living correctly, not burning up chemical elements faster than they can be replaced, under normal circumstances, and under the proper diet. These supplements are needed to make up what we especially lack from the "average" American dietary habits.

Supplements should be used daily in the diet and served at the dining table. They help counteract the shortages found in the common diet today. Also add them to liquefied drinks, salads, or even desserts.

Acidophilus culture: Lactobacillus acidophilus in capsule or liquid form aids in controlling undesirable bowel bacteria, reducing putrefaction, and keeping the bowel clean.

Alfalfa tablets: Alfalfa, rich in chlorophyll and fiber, helps maintain bowel health through the natural cleansing action of chlorophyll and quickened bowel transit time from the fiber.

Beet tablets: Good for sluggish liver and gallbladder, this supplement gently stimulates bowel regularity.

Bee pollen: Rich in lecithin, bee pollen is 20 percent protein and contains all known essential vitamins, twelve essential minerals and trace elements, bioflavonoids, enzymes, complex sugars, plant steroids, and ten fatty acids. Bee pollen increases stamina and quickens recovery time from athletic exertion or physical labor.

Blackstrap molasses (unsulfured): If you can find a health food store that has it, buy it. Molasses is the "residue" from processing sugar beets and sugar cane into pure granulated sugar (sucrose). It is loaded with vitamins and minerals. You can take it straight by spoonfuls or add it to other foods. (Not all molasses in the markets is the real thing. Always read the labels.)

Brewer's yeast: A great natural source of B-complex (except B_{12}) and other vitamins, brewer's yeast is high in amino acids and minerals. Because it is high in phosphorus (which requires calcium for balance), brewer's yeast should always be taken with a generous helping of yogurt or other high-calcium food.

Carob: Chocolate-flavored powder made from finely ground legume pods from carob trees. Carob is more nutritious than cocoa and has no caffeine.

Chlorophyll: This wonderful natural cleanser is rich in magnesium and is in all green vegetables, especially the leafy vegetables. It is available in liquid form in health food stores and is very high in the edible algae spirulina and chlorella.

Chlorella: This is a very popular supplement in Asian countries. Chlorella is an edible alga loaded with nutrients and especially noted for a complex protein growth factor that aids in healing damaged tissues. It helps rid the body of heavy metals and other toxins. Chlorella supports the liver and enhances the immune system.

Cod liver oil: Still the all-around best source of vitamins A and D.

Dulse: I recommend Nova Scotia dulse, but if you can't find it, any dulse will supply iodine for the thyroid gland.

Flaxseed (meal): Flaxseed contains omega-3 fatty acids and is the best vegetarian source of fiber. It should be kept refrigerated. Grind it finely and add a little (I mean "a little," like half a teaspoon) to fruit and vegetable juices. Too much will cause the juice to thicken. (It can also be sprinkled on hot or cold cereal.) Omega-3 fatty acids help protect people from heart attacks, and the fiber not only quickens bowel transit time but carries off cholesterol and triglycerides that would normally be assimilated from the bowel into the lymph.

Ginseng: Chinese herbalists regard ginseng (powdered ginseng root) as one of the best (if not the very best) all-around, health-supporting "tonics." It is most effective in the form of tea. Many ginseng users believe it enhances their sex life. I believe *anything* that enhances your health will enhance your sex life.

Herb teas: Fenugreek, comfrey, peppermint, lemon grass, spearmint, chamomile, oat straw (you have to boil this one for five minutes), and red raspberry are all wonderful herb teas. Visit the tea section of your supermarket and check out all the wonderful herb teas they now carry.

Milk substitutes: The variety of healthy, nutrient-rich substitutes for cow's milk is growing and includes raw nut and seed milks, soy milk, and rice milk.

Niacin: Taking a gram of this B-complex vitamin with every meal can cut down the liver's production of cholesterol and can bring blood to the head, improving oxygen supply to the brain. If you want to try it, start with 100 milligrams of niacin to see how well you tolerate the upper body and facial flush that comes with it. Increase by 100 milligrams more each week until you are taking 1,000 milligrams (same as 1 gram) with each meal. Consult your doctor before you try it.

Oat bran: Oat bran offers soluble and insoluble fiber which shortens bowel transit time and reduces blood levels of triglycerides and cholesterol. You can sprinkle it on your cereal, salads, or soups; add it to bread, muffin, or bagel recipes; or just take a tablespoonful three times a day or so.

Omega-3 fatty acids: You can get them from eating fish or flaxseed oil. Eskimos survive on a high-fat diet but have a very low incidence of heart disease, because they get a lot of omega-3 oils by eating a lot of fish. You can do the same by using flaxseed oil.

Rice bran syrup: Similar to molasses, this syrup adds a great flavor to goat milk, rice or soy milk, and raw nut or seed milk. It is loaded with vitamins and minerals, especially silicon.

Rice polishings (same as bran): Same nutrients as rice bran syrup but not as nutrient dense.

RNA (ribonucleic acid): This specialized nucleic acid is called "the long life factor," and is found most abundantly in chlorella, canned sardines, and brewer's yeast.

Spirulina: An edible alga harvested from lakes in Latin America and in Africa, spirulina is high in chlorophyll and B-complex vitamins. Some is being grown commercially in the United States under controlled conditions to produce the most nutrient-rich spirulina possible.

Wheat germ/wheat germ oil: Best natural source of vitamin E for fighting free radicals; it aids energy production, and it protects pituitary and adrenal hormones.

Whey: Goat milk whey is one of the best sources of bioorganic sodium and potassium I have ever found, not to mention that it carries a handful of essential minerals or trace elements.

Supplements don't have to be in pill form. A person has to be in good health to assimilate "pill" form supplements. The supplements just discussed can be assimilated by anyone, even though they are concentrated. Use them in cereals, tonics, drinks, dressings, and almost any recipe. However, heat and baking break down lecithin, many vitamins, and minerals.

MORE HELPFUL FOOD AND MEALTIME TIPS

Because you are unique, there are most probably specific ways to enhance your weight-loss program that will work very well for you but not necessarily well for others. The reverse is also true. Don't get too excited when a friend "shares" some great new dieting or weight-loss rumor from the grapevine at a family fitness center, aerobics class, or health food store. Be open minded but be very cautious.

One tip that has helped many people is to take four capsules or tablets of chlorella or spirulina half an hour before mealtime. Another is to take a heaping teaspoon of bee pollen fifteen minutes before eating. Either one may reduce your appetite.

Apple cider vinegar and honey in a glass of water has helped some individuals lose weight. Add 1 tablespoon of apple cider vinegar and ½ teaspoon of honey to 16 ounces of water. Take this morning and evening.

Limit your fat intake to what you get in foods such as avocado, eggs, and nut and seed butters. Be careful with salad dressings; most are very high in calories.

Make sure you are getting enough iodine to keep your metabolism up and enough vitamin E to help get oxygen to the brain. Use at least ½ teaspoon of dulse flakes every day, or a dulse tablet with morning and evening meals. People under age forty should take 400 units of vitamin E per day, and people over forty should increase that to 800 units. If you are using wheat germ oil, you don't need the vitamin E. There is vitamin E in the wheat germ oil.

You may want to use niacin to flush the toxins from organs and peripheral tissues, speed up the elimination process, and reduce production of cholesterol by the liver. Start with 100 milligrams at each meal and work up to 500 milligrams. From 100 to 500 milligrams, add 50 milligrams to the 100 milligrams every four days until you are taking a total of 1,000 milligrams. Niacin is vitamin B_3, perfectly safe but uncomfortable to some because of the release of histamines that cause the face, ears, and neck to redden and tingle for fifteen minutes to half an hour. The histaminic response is accompanied by a flushing of blood capillaries and increased circulation.

DR. JENSEN'S EXTREME HUNGER SNACK

I call this my *Special Slim Shake,* and it can be used as a substitute for one or two meals each day because it is such a great building food, with only about half as many calories as a diet meal.

SPECIAL SLIM SHAKE RECIPE
(185 CALORIES)

1 tablespoon skim milk powder, soy powder, whey, or nut powder

1 tablespoon bee pollen

1 teaspoon chlorella granules or 6 tablets

1 sliver avocado or ½ banana

1 cup apple juice or 1½ tablespoons apple concentrate in 1 cup of water

Combine ingredients in blender and blend for 1 minute. Whey can be substituted for the skim milk powder to help develop the friendly bowel flora. This formula builds the red blood cell count; keeps up the blood sugar level; supplies trace elements; provides amino acids, fatty acids, and fiber; and is high in chlorophyll for cleansing the tissues.

CHAPTER 7

WHAT TO EXPECT
AS YOU IMPROVE

One of the wonderful advantages of my
diet plan is that weight loss is accompa-
nied by a gradual normalizing of the body chemistry as mineral and vitamin deficiencies are taken care of and as
appropriate ratios of protein, carbohydrate, and fat from high-
quality foods begin to change the body.

The human body is in constant change. Old cells die and
new cells grow to take their places. Over a period of a year or
so, most of the chemical elements of which we are made are
replaced. We are physically renewed. Whether there is any
improvement in this new body over the old one depends on
you—what you have put into your mouth and what you have
done with your body during that year.

The best attitude to develop is a positive expectation that
proper nutrition and exercise are going to create the best body
you could possibly have. You're going to feel better, enjoy
yourself more, sleep better, have more energy, move more

quickly and gracefully, and enjoy your work more. You will think more quickly and clearly. Begin to appreciate how your body feels. When you become sensitized to what makes your body and mind work better, you'll be more sensitive about what you put into them.

When you go through my diet plan and follow my Health and Harmony Food Regimen, your body will be replacing old tissue with better-quality tissue. This will result in physical effects that the average person wouldn't experience on an average diet, but as you move to a better, more natural diet, you will move in the direction of better health. Initially, you'll have less energy as the body adapts to its lower weight. Later, you'll have more energy, vitality, and zest for life.

As your body is cleansed and renewed, you may experience disturbances that you don't understand or like. When heavy, habitual use of coffee, tea, chocolate, or cola drinks is stopped, headaches and depression may occur. This is because the removal of caffeine and other chemicals unnatural to the body creates a temporary imbalance in the blood chemistry, which registers in the brain as a headache. Usually the body is detoxified in three days and the symptoms vanish.

Sometimes, however, our bodies, due to poor living habits and environmental pollutants, have accumulated more toxic substances and have developed more imbalances than we realize, particularly when suppressant medications have been taken in response to colds, flu, hay fever, bronchitis, asthma, arthritis, and other disturbances and diseases. Fatty tissue, particularly, tends to store toxic debris and heavy metals. When toxic drug residues, old catarrh, heavy metals, and other substances are released from tissues in the processes of cleansing and renewal, we may experience a temporary *healing crisis,* which acts very much like disease conditions. Knowing what to expect will remove much of the anxiety at encountering these situations.

THE REVERSAL PROCESS

In contrast to current myths about *catching* diseases, most, if not all, chronic diseases are the natural result of unnatural lifestyle habits. We eat, drink, worry, and think them into existence. We put junk food and alcohol into the fatigued body, then stay up till all hours "having a good time." We fight with our spouses, then go to bed with nerve acids and adrenaline eating us up. We work at stressful jobs day after day, pour down coffee, fight traffic on the freeway, and watch the latest unpleasant news on TV—crime, war, disaster, and so forth. All of this has its effects on the body—*negative effects.*

We come down with colds and flu, which are actually natural cleansing processes, and because we don't want the symptoms, we take powerful cold medications that suppress certain brain centers, stop the elimination of catarrh and toxic wastes, and block the body's natural ways of taking care of these things. Catarrh and toxins become locked into the tissue structure where they serve as more or less permanent irritants, degrading the surrounding tissue. Blocking natural cleansing processes like colds and flu sets up preconditions for more serious breakdowns and diseases later.

If we interrupt this pattern by shifting to a natural lifestyle, eating good food, exercising, and taking care of our bodies, many things change inside the body. With the right nutrients available, body energies shift to assist internal organs in repairing themselves. We may feel tired and experience lowered vitality, but it is only temporary. Wonderful things are happening in the body. Our energy is being used for tissue rebuilding, so less of it is available for ordinary life tasks. But it will return, with interest. This phase may last from ten days to two weeks.

Weight loss as developed in my program is a reversal process, reversing the accumulation of fatty tissue that contains toxic encumbrances. *Your health will improve as a result of it.*

As tissues in organ after organ are rebuilt, and long-term vitamin and mineral deficiencies are taken care of, the metabolic level is increased. This, at some point, gives the tissues enough strength to start getting rid of some of those toxic wastes we have forced into them. This is usually a very rewarding weight-loss period. There may be increased kidney and bowel elimination for a while before the body stabilizes.

It is especially important to take care of the urinary system during a time of elimination, and there are special foods, drinks, vitamins, minerals, and herbs that help us cleanse and rejuvenate the kidneys, as shown in the following list.

Urinary System

Structure: Kidneys, bladder, ureters, urethra.

Function: Elimination of liquid waste; regulation of chemical composition of blood, fluid, and electrolyte balance and volume; maintenance of acid-base balance.

Foods: Watermelon (including seeds), pomegranate, apples, asparagus, liquid chlorophyll, parsley, green leafy vegetables.

Drinks: Celery/pomegranate juice, black currant juice/juniper berry tea, pomegranate juice/goat whey, celery/parsley/asparagus juice, beet juice, grapes; KB-11 tea, cleaver tea.

Vitamins: A, B-complex, C, D, E, choline, pantothenic acid.

Minerals: Calcium, potassium, manganese, silicon, iron, chlorine, magnesium.

Herbs: Juniper berries, uva ursi, parsley, goldenseal, slippery elm, elderflowers, ginger, dandelion, marshmallow.

The weight may stabilize or even increase for a time, but don't worry. More building and repair is going on inside the body at a faster rate. Even though you are on a lower-calorie diet than before, your digestion and assimilation are so much better that food is more efficiently used.

THE HEALING CRISIS

When you are feeling great, suddenly a healing crisis will erupt. If you have had boils or skin problems in the past, they may return. Colds, flu, fever, diarrhea—discharges from any or all orifices of the body—may occur. The body is retracing its way back to health, and it stops at each point in the past where you have had some ailment or disease, which was incompletely taken care of, and the same old symptoms return. Old, stored toxic material is discharged. Again, this is a wonderful thing, although it can be most uncomfortable at the time. This is nature's way of healing, extremely thorough. Don't try to stop it with medication. It will stop itself in from three days to a week or so.

Symptoms experienced during the healing crisis depend on how well you have treated your body and on what ailments you have had in the past. The reversal process usually takes you from one ailment to another (over a period of time), in reverse order of their appearance, so you experience the symptoms of the most recent ailment or disease first.

After the healing crisis, you'll feel great again. But that doesn't mean it's all over. You may go through several crises in the coming months and years, until all the old debris of past illnesses is cleansed out of your system. Once it is gone, it is permanently gone and you do not have to experience any of those old troubles again if you are living right.

You may lose considerable weight during a healing crisis, but you will gain only part of it back. It may stabilize for ten days to two weeks after that, or you may continue losing weight as you stick to your diet.

KEEP TRACK OF YOUR PROGRESS

It is an excellent idea to see a doctor who knows nutrition before you start on a diet. It is a must if you are over fifty years old or more than 10 pounds overweight, or if you have any chronic disease or physical condition that might be negatively affected by diet and exercise changes. I believe that my reducing program is safe to use with almost any state of health, but you must check with your doctor to be sure.

You may want to ask your doctor for the SMA Panel test to have some basis for checking your state of health and progress at suitable intervals.

CHAPTER 8

TIPS ON STAYING AT THE RIGHT WEIGHT

When you reach the weight that is natural for you, it will take fewer calories to keep you going than when you were overweight, with a few extra allowed to meet the needs of your exercise program. Weigh yourself once a week, and if you find your weight has crept up more than 3 pounds, *lose it*. You will know how by the time you finish this book.

Eat a wide variety of foods you like, based on my Health and Harmony Food Regimen, as presented in chapter 6.

Remember, permanent lifestyle changes are the key to keeping slim and fit. These include changes in attitude, thinking, exercise, recreation, eating habits, and anything else that has contributed to your gaining excess weight in the past. Buy new clothes that fit the new you, and enjoy the way you look and feel wearing them.

CHANGING FOOD HABITS

1. Cut sugar and white flour products to a minimum. Sugar drains vitamins from body reserves, throws calcium and the endocrine system out of balance, and adds worthless calories to the diet. White flour has had most of its food value removed during processing and bleaching, slows intestinal activities (which encourages weight gain), and is easily broken down to worthless sugar calories in the body.

2. Cut down processed foods. Their food value is reduced in processing, and chemical additives in them may cause chemical imbalances or toxic reactions in the body.

3. Cut down salt or use a little evaporated sea salt instead. Salt causes water retention and has been linked to hypertension and other diseases. Try herbs, broth powder, and natural seasonings instead. Eat foods high in potassium, which helps to eliminate excess water from the body.

4. Throw away the frying pan. Avoid all fat-fried foods and foods cooked in hot grease or oil.

5. Eat at mealtimes with your family. You can eat what they do, only eat less than you used to eat. Always leave some food on the plate to train your mind to exercise discipline over appetite.

6. Realize that feeling hungry does not mean you should immediately snack on something. Hungs pangs and thirst are often confused. Try drinking a glass of water to see if hunger disappears.

7. Those who tend to hold water—the hydripheric types—should eat high-potassium foods often (see Table 8.1). Cleaver tea, KB-11, and vitamin B_6 will help reduce water retention. It is also important to have adequate intake levels of vitamin B_{12} and iron.

Table 8.1. **Ten Foods Highest in Potassium**

Food	(Milligrams per 100-gram portion)
Molasses (blackstrap)	2,927
Yeast, torula	2,046
Yeast, bakers', dry, active	1,998
Soy flour	1,730
Soybeans, dry, raw	1,677
Apricots, dried	1,561
Lima beans, dry, raw	1,499
Rice bran, dry, raw	1,495
Peaches, dried	1,191
Wheat bran, dry, raw	1,050

8. Cut down on fat-rich foods and alcoholic beverages. Obvious sources of high-fat foods are whole milk, whole milk cheese, cream, butter, cream cheese, sour cream, fried foods, margarine, mayonnaise, many salad dressings, pork products (especially bacon), duck, ground meat, frankfurters, and spare ribs. Not so obvious sources include avocados, chocolate, coconut, nuts, and seeds.

9. Plan ahead on how you will handle holiday meals at your home or with relatives. You can simply control your eating, or you may wish to skip or skimp on another meal or two so that you can consume more at the holiday meal.

CHANGING YOUR BEHAVIOR

Unless your motivation and behavior are in line with your goals, the best diet plan in the world will do you no good. My diet plan is designed for mature adults who are willing to make the necessary changes in lifestyle to bring down their weight and keep it where it belongs. According to the research of Dr. Albert J Stunkard, there are five basic steps to increase your chances of success in losing weight.

1. Keep daily records of what you eat and how much you exercise.
2. Watch out for places, events, and times that stimulate a desire to snack, and change them as necessary. If you have always snacked before bedtime, for example, try doing a crossword puzzle or having a cup of herb tea instead. Don't try to simply suppress old habits; exchange them for better ones.
3. Change the way you eat, especially if you tend to gobble down food as you work or perform some other activity— such as reading or watching TV. When you eat, do nothing else but eat. Look at your food, savor it, enjoy each bite. Learn to be emotionally satisfied with it. When we rush through meals unconscious of our food, it is all too easy to overeat.
4. Reward yourself for successful weight loss or for maintaining a healthy weight. Buy something you've wanted for a while, or go to the movies or a concert. It doesn't have to be a big thing. You can buy a little box of gold stars at a variety store and make up a score sheet where you give yourself a gold star each week for meeting your goals.
5. Be positive about your life changes. Avoid feeling sorry for yourself that you can't gorge on food any more, and concentrate on how much better you feel and look. *Avoid negative feelings about yourself and your weight.* Find good things to say and think. Take life a day at a time

until you have maintained your natural weight steadily for six months.

I would like to add that we should always drink two 8-ounce glasses of water half an hour before each meal. Thirst and hunger signals often overlap, and if you don't drink water first, you are more likely to overeat.

We find that brain centers that have become adjusted to unhealthy habits may take months to adjust to a new lifestyle. This doesn't mean you will be tortured with hunger pangs during the intervening period, it only means you will have to exercise some prudence and caution.

If you are used to watching TV and drinking beer or eating peanuts when you come home from work, try taking a short nap or exercising instead. Get involved in more active things than you were before. Go roller-skating, see a baseball game or a ballet, take hikes, play tennis or raquetball with a friend. Try to find some activity that helps lift others, and volunteer time for it.

The basic idea here is that sometimes food unconsciously becomes higher on our priority list of life events than it should be. When we stop and think about how much time, energy, and money we put into food and food-related events, we may be very surprised, realizing that it is time to reevaluate what is really important in life. Then we can begin adding new activities and dropping old ones to make changes in accordance with our new priorities.

CHAPTER 9

TWO DIET PLANS FOR LOSING WEIGHT, KEEPING FIT, AND STAYING HEALTHY

I n this chapter, I am going to present my Special Two-Week Diet Plan and my Thirty-Day Diet Plan with two meal options, one for 1,200 calories per day, the other for 1,800 calories, each one nutritionally balanced. The fat content in both diets is sharply reduced since no fried or deep-fat-fried foods are allowed, and the use of fats and oils in meals is minimized. The American average daily intake of fat is 35 to 40 percent of the diet, which many doctors and nutritionists consider much more than we should be getting. I have recommended a low-fat food regimen for over fifty years to my patients. You will get adequate amounts of fat from the meat, fish, poultry, dairy products, nuts, and seeds in my diet plan, and it is well under 30 percent of dietary calories.

I recommend that physically active but overweight men and women (those who work at physically demanding jobs, who have a great deal of work to do at home, and who exercise hard and regularly) try the 1,800-calorie diet if they need to lose weight. Less active people should try the 1,200-calorie diet.

People with chronic weight problems of many years' standing should see a doctor, as we have mentioned previously that it could be an endocrine problem, which needs more specialized assistance. Those who always gain after dieting, especially when living healthy, need to seek out a nutritional counselor. Exercise is usually recommended to prevent weight gain.

Nutritional researchers recommend that women avoid diets under 1,000 calories a day and that men avoid diets under 1,500 calories, but both men and women whose lifestyle is more sedentary, more on the slow-and-easy side, will be all right on the 1,200-calorie diet. If you are in doubt, check with your doctor and show him or her my diet plan. But make sure he or she knows something about nutrition so you'll be getting sound advice, not worthless opinion.

THE SECRET OF MY DIET PLAN

The secret of my diet plan lies as much in what is not in it as what is there. The primary benefit, I believe, comes from two factors: plenty of healthy fresh vegetables and fruits and reduction of fats, proteins, and refined carbohydrates. You will notice there are no jams, jellies, pies, cakes, cola drinks, or chips and dips in my diet plan. Refined white sugar, white flour products, and most packaged, refined products are left out for reasons given in previous chapters. Pork is left out. Fatty meats and manufactured meat products such as sausage and hot dogs are out. Butter is minimized. Whole, pure, natural, fresh foods are emphasized.

In an experiment, three groups of Swedish athletes were put on three different diets (high-protein and fat diet, mixed diet, high–complex carbohydrate diet) for three days, then given a bicycle-riding endurance test. The athletes on the complex carbohydrate diet, mostly fruit, vegetables, whole grain bread, and cereal grains, outperformed the others by going three hours, as compared to two hours for the mixed diet group and one hour for the high-protein group. My diet is also high in complex carbohydrates, which means it is more sustaining than most other diets.

You see, your body molds to what you put in it. Eating junk food builds a junk body. The body does its best with what you feed it, but the only way it can protest against wrong eating habits is by getting fatigued, sick, fat, or unattractively thin. That is something to stop and think about.

Another secret of my diet plan is cutting back a little on protein, cutting back a lot on fats, increasing the complex carbohydrates, and cutting out refined carbohydrates. There is plenty of fiber in my diet plan and lots of natural vitamins and minerals, and you will find variety and simplicity in the foods recommended.

DON'T BE FOOLED BY MYTHS

Don't be fooled by that old myth that says vegetables and meat without salt are drab, boring, and tasteless. Nothing could be farther from the truth, and you have some wonderful surprises in store.

Go to your local health food store and see what it has in the way of natural vegetable and herbal seasonings. Some of these are absolutely wonderful, with a satisfying salty taste.

Don't try to cheat by using salt substitutes (I think they are worse than salt), by using lots of salted butter, or by using white rice and other quick-cooking substitutes for the natural grains in the diet plan. You'll only be cheating yourself of nutritional value and of the wonderful discoveries you'll be making by honestly trying to change eating habits. You can use a little sea salt—but go easy on it. Salt holds water in the body.

Now, I am not telling you that food will not taste different, even somewhat bland, when you first switch to your new diet. It will take a week or two for your taste buds to get rid of that burned-out quality due to heavy salt and spice use in the past. Then, what you eat will begin to taste wonderful.

WHAT ABOUT HERBS?

I often caution patients about spices and spicy foods because they tend to be hard on the liver. Many spices irritate the gastrointestinal tract. The wonderful thing about herbs is that they not only enhance flavor but contain vitamins, minerals, and other nutrients that contribute to better health. And we find the great majority of them are extremely low in calories and are absolutely safe.

HERBS TO DELIGHT THE TASTE

Anise leaves, with a light, sweet licorice flavor, are very nice in salads, or on fish and poultry.

Basil, one of the most popular herbs used in cooking, is excellent in salads, soups, sauces, meats, and stuffing. Use fresh leaves of sweet basil if available.

Bay leaves make a tasty addition to soups, stews, and roasts.

Borage, a large flowering plant greatly loved by honeybees, has a light, cucumber-like taste. Use young leaves and flowers in salads.

Burnet is good in salads, similar in taste to borage. The chopped leaves are good in soups and sauces. The finest French dressings are flavored with burnet.

Caraway leaves in vegetable, fish, and meat dishes are very good; the seeds are sometimes used in bread.

Chervil, called the "gourmet's parsley," enhances the taste of other seasonings and has a unique flavor of its own. Use in soups, salads, and sauces.

Chives are familiar to most, but if you haven't used them, try cutting them into soups, salads, sauces, or onto any food whose taste would be enhanced by a mild onion flavor. Many people like chives on baked potatoes.

Coriander leaves, fresh, are not widely available outside the Southwest where many supermarkets carry them, but you can grow your own easily from seed. For a cool, distinctive flavor, try them on fish, in salads, soups, stews, sauces, and vegetables, and virtually any main dish.

Costmary or "Bible leaf" was put in books in days past to keep out silverfish. It is a nice herb for salads, teas, meat, poultry, and fish chowder.

Dill leaves are good in tuna or chicken salad, while the seeds are sometimes used in bread, omelets, meat, poultry, and herb butters.

Gotu kola, familiar to many as an Oriental medicinal herb, makes a tasty salad green.

Lemongrass makes a lovely tea, especially delicious as an iced tea on hot summer days.

Lemon verbena, one of the most fragrant herbs, is a nice addition to fruit salads and fruit drinks.

Licorice mint, strongly flavored, is good in fruit salads.

Marjoram is a standard seasoning herb from a small bush. Try it fresh in salads or with tomato slices or in soups, sauces, meat dishes, and fish. Sweet marjoram is the best seasoning for soups and sauces.

Mint leaves (fresh) are lovely in salads. Spearmint is a favorite seasoning for lamb.

Oregano is another of the very popular herbs. Almost any food flavor is enhanced with oregano. Greek oregano, new to many in this country, has a stronger flavor.

Parsley is a nice addition to soups, salads, sauces, and omelets. It is loaded with vitamin A and other vitamins.

Rosemary is another popular herb. Just a sprig in soups, stews, and sauces adds a nice flavor.

Sage creates a lovely savory taste when added to eggs, soups, fish, meat, and stuffing. This is another well-known seasoning.

Savory, once called "poor man's pepper," adds zing to soups, sauces, and salads. Use only a sprig or less until you've sampled the flavor. Summer savory is preferred in salads, while winter savory is considered wonderful with green beans.

Sorrel (French) has a somewhat sour flavor and is nice in salads or cooked with spinach or chard.

Tarragon (French) is used to flavor vinegar. Fresh tarragon has ten times as much flavor as the dried variety.

Thyme, a small-leafed plant with a marvelous fragrance, is used in salad dressings, stuffings, omelets, sauces, and with meats and eggs. English thyme is the most popular, while French thyme is milder.

Watercress, a nice salad green, is surprisingly high in vitamins, minerals (especially potassium), and even protein. Potassium helps keep water absorption down in those who tend to hold too much water in their tissues.

I strongly encourage you to experiment with herbs in your cooked and fresh raw foods. It's a whole new, lovely world, and you won't be disappointed.

VEGETARIAN DIETS AND HEALTH

Research has shown that vegans (no eggs, no milk, no animal products) and vegetarians (may use eggs or milk or both) have lower blood levels of cholesterol and triglycerides than meat eaters. A vegetarian diet is not for everyone, but for those whose lifestyles and personal preferences permit it, vegetarianism may be the healthiest way to live—and the slimmest.

Let me pause for a word of caution. The reason I use the phrase "for those whose lifestyles and personal preferences permit it" is because there is more to vegetarianism than meets the eye. I do not believe vegetarianism is consistent with a high-stress job or lifestyle. I think it is difficult to be a vegetarian in a fast-paced, conflict-ridden environment. Vegetarianism requires a peaceful and harmonious way of life, and if you are not prepared to live that way, you may not be ready to be a vegetarian. It is also unrealistic, if you have enjoyed and eaten meat for many years, to make an intellectual decision to suddenly switch to vegetables strictly for health reasons. I'm not saying it is impossible, but it is very difficult. I recommend *The Vegan Sourcebook* by Joanne Stepaniak for those who want to know more about this way of life.

I must also warn that overeating vegetarian foods can lead to obesity just as overeating nonvegetarian foods does. The same principle applies. If you take in more calories than you use every day, the excess calories will be stored as fat.

LET'S HAVE A CLOSER LOOK AT VEGETARIANISM

Although no reliable census has been taken, a 1992 survey by the Vegetarian Resource Group in Baltimore, Maryland, found that 12.5 million Americans called themselves vegetarians, while millions of others deliberately limit their use of meat and poultry. In the past, the main questions regarding vegetarianism were centered around whether you could get enough protein, vitamin B_{12}, and iron from such a diet. Many cases of deficiencies were found among vegetarians in decades past, but times have changed.

Enough is now known about nutrition to allow planning a diet that provides sufficient amounts of all nutrients, even for fast-growing children.

A twenty-year study of Seventh-Day Adventists by Dr. Roland Phillips and Dr. David Snowden has turned up some interesting health facts. About half of this religious denomination is made up of lacto-ovo-vegetarians, which means they use eggs and milk products as well as vegetables, grains, and fruits. The two doctors found that older men who ate meat six times a week or more were twice as likely to die of heart disease than older men who did not eat meat. Middle-aged meat eaters were four times more likely to die of heart attacks than non-meat eaters in the same age group. Seventh-Day Adventists have lower rates of cancer of the breast, ovaries, prostate, and pancreas; they are half as likely to develop cancer of the colon or rectum. Only 15 percent of the vegetarian Adventists are overweight, compared to 30 to 40 percent of the meat eaters. In the American population as a whole, 60 percent are considered overweight. Strict vegetarians who do not eat eggs or milk products tend to be the leanest because they get less fat and more low-calorie vegetables and fiber.

Studies in Italy have shown that soy protein lowers blood cholesterol better than a low-fat, low-cholesterol diet. A study in Israel indicated a low 2 percent of vegetarians had high blood pressure, compared with 26 percent of nonvegetarians. Researchers from Australia found that when meat users changed to a diet of vegetables, milk, and eggs for six weeks, their blood pressure dropped. When they returned to their normal meat-eating routine, it went up again. A Boston study, in which 8 ounces of meat was added daily to the diets of strict vegetarians, showed an increase in blood cholesterol of 19 percent.

We find a decisive lowering of cancer and heart disease among vegetarians, but there is some debate as to the true reason. Dr. Alex Hershaft points out that not only does meat contain saturated fat and cholesterol but often pesticides, hormones, and residual antibiotics from the cattle feed as well. Toxic substances like these are concentrated twenty times higher in the fatty tissue as in the meat. (One of the best reasons for reducing is that toxins and heavy metals are concentrated in human fat, too.) It is probable that the toxins in the

animal fat, nonexistent before the twentieth century, play a sig-
nificant role in the genesis and growth of chronic disease in
meat eaters.

What about getting enough protein from vegetarian
foods? For one thing, the egg is the most efficiently matched
protein to the needs of the human body. It has all the nutrients
required to make life, including all eight amino acids essential
to human nutrition. It is also possible, by combining certain
vegetarian foods, to make a complete protein out of two foods
deficient in one or more of the amino acids. These must be
eaten at the same meal. (See Table 9.1.)

For example, bread is deficient in two essential amino
acids, but if it is eaten with cheese, the combination is a much
higher quality protein than either alone. Dairy products and
grain products are, generally speaking, an excellent combined
protein. Since Americans use so much milk and wheat in their
daily diets, it is best to limit these in a vegetarian diet to avoid
excess catarrh and possible allergies. Try to use other grains
often, and use wheat only once in a while. Milk and milk
products also supply the amino acids that are deficient in seeds,
nuts, beans, and potatoes.

Legumes mainly lack the amino acid tryptophan and those
amino acids containing sulfur. Tofu, which is soybean curd, is
deficient only in the sulfur amino acids (as are soybeans).
Grains complement legumes almost perfectly. Good combinations include:

Soybeans, rice, wheat
Soybeans, peanuts, sesame seeds
Soybeans, wheat, sesame seeds

Table 9.1. **Vegetarian Foods Highest in Protein**

Food	(Percent of Food as Protein)	Food	(Percent of Food as Protein)
Soy grits, low fat	47.3	Wheat bran	14.6
Gluten flour	41.4	Brazil nuts, raw	14.3★
Brewer's yeast	38.8	Cottage cheese,	
Soy flour	38.6	creamed	13.3
Soy milk, dry	34.1	Rice bran	13.3
Pignolia nuts, raw	31.1	Whey powder	12.9
Pumpkin seeds, raw	29.0	Hazelnuts, raw	12.6
Swiss cheese	28.8	Eggs, whole	12.5
Peanuts, raw	26.5	Rye, grain	12.1
Peanuts, roasted	26.4★	Rye, flour	11.9
Wheat germ	26.3	Buckwheat	11.7
Sunflower seeds, raw	24.0	Whole wheat flour	11.5★
Garbanzo beans	20.5	Pasta	11.5
Almonds, raw	19.5	Soybeans, cooked	11.0★
Pistachios, raw	19.3	White flour	11.0★
Sesame seeds, raw	18.6	Miso	10.5
Cottage cheese,		Wheat, whole grain	10.2★
uncreamed	18.2	Millet, whole grain	9.9
Cashews, raw	17.2	Cornmeal, dry	9.2
Ricotta cheese	16.7	Cream cheese	9.0★
Egg yolks	16.2	Cracked wheat bread	8.5★
Walnuts, raw	14.8	Boiled lima beans	8.2★

★High in fats or carbohydrates.

Soybeans, corn, milk
Legumes and rice
Beans and wheat
Beans and corn
Beans and milk
Rice and wheat

Vegetables tend to lack sulfur-containing amino acids, so to increase their protein value we could serve them with sesame seeds, millet, rice, or mushrooms (all high in the sulfur amino acids). Vegetarians should consider having bread, cornbread, or a cereal grain with salads or other vegetable dishes to enhance protein value.

HOW FATTENING IS CHEESE?

When we look at how cheese is made, we find out that whey is taken out and it is not a true "whole" food. Whey is high in natural sodium, wonderful for the digestive system and joints, but in cheese this natural sodium is replaced with table salt sodium, which is not good for us.

I feel that cheese is still one of our better proteins, considering the other proteins available to us, but we need to realize we have to be careful in selecting cheese, like any other food.

Because of the salt and saturated fats in cheese, we should know it is fattening if used too much. Cheese is a good cell-building, cell-repairing food, but it is not a perfect food, so we must be careful to use it in moderation.

A vegetarian reducing diet can be used just as easily as one containing meat, and it will reduce blood cholesterol and triglycerides more rapidly. Care must be taken to get sufficient protein, iron, and vitamin B_{12}. (See Tables 9.2, 9.3, and 9.4.) Arrange meals so that each day the calorie count is at least 1,000 calories for women, 1,500 calories for men, with about 16 percent protein, 64 percent carbohydrates, and 20 percent fat. Sufficient fat is generally available if eggs, whole grains, nuts, and seeds are included each day. Most raw nuts and seeds are over 50 percent vegetable lipids, the healthiest kind, with no cholesterol.

Table 9.2. **Fat Levels in Cheese**	
Low Saturated Fat	*(Grams per Ounce)*
Dry-curd cottage cheese	0.08
Low-fat cottage cheese, 1%	0.18
Low-fat cottage cheese, 2%	0.35
Creamed cottage cheese	0.81
Part-skim ricotta	1.38
Moderate Saturated Fat	
Whole-milk ricotta	2.32
Part-skim mozzarella	2.87
Low-moisture, part-skim mozzarella	3.08
Mozzarella	3.73
American pasteurized process cheese spread	3.78
High Saturated Fat	
Neufchatel	4.20
Feta	4.24
Camembert	4.33
American pasteurized process cheese food	4.38
Low-moisture mozzarella	4.41
Hard Parmesan	4.65
Port duSalut	4.73
	(Continued)

Table 9.2. **Continued**

High Saturated Fat	
Limburger	4.75
Tilsit	4.76
Provolone	4.84
Edam	4.98
Gouda	4.99
Swiss	5.04
Blue	5.30
Brick	5.32
Gruyere	5.36
Grated Parmesan	5.41
Muenster	5.42
Gjetost	5.43
Fontina	5.44
Roquefort	5.46
Pimento (pasteurized process)	5.57
American (pasteurized process)	5.58
Colby	5.73
Cheddar	5.98
Cream cheese	6.23

Keep in mind that a vegetarian diet is not for everyone. Those who want to try this regimen might consider easing into it gradually. Just cutting out meat does not make a balanced vegetarian regimen. Vegetarianism is a mental discipline as well as a food regimen, and many vegetarians practice it for ethical or spiritual reasons. To many, vegetarianism is associated with a philosophy of pacifism, or even peaceful coexistence with all life. It can take ten years for the body to adjust to a vegetarian diet, and

Table 9.3. **Foods High in Iron**

Food	(Milligrams per 100 Grams)
Rice bran, dry	20.5
Brewer's yeast	17.3
Blackstrap molasses	16.1
Pumpkin seeds	11.2
Sesame seeds	10.5
Wheat germ	9.9
Soy grits	9.3
Soy flour	7.4
Pistachio nuts	7.3
Sunflower seeds	7.1
Millet	6.8
Parsley	6.5

Table 9.4. **Foods High in Vitamin B$_{12}$**

Food	(Milligrams per 100 Grams)
Cheese	1
Egg yolk	6
Kelp	N/A
Milk	N/A
Eggs, whole	2
Dried whey	2

★ 6 micrograms needed per day

there are some who will never be vegetarians because the lifestyle they have chosen is incompatible with vegetarianism.

VARIETY IS ESSENTIAL

One of the greatest things I can tell you about diet, health, and nutrition is that a variety of good foods is essential. Variety will help you lose weight and stay at the weight you should be. Variety helps guarantee that the vitamins, minerals, enzymes, proteins, carbohydrates, and lipids you need to feed the brain, nerves, glands, muscles, bones, teeth, and vital organs will be sufficient to keep you fit and full of vitality. Variety reduces the need for supplementary vitamins and minerals and cuts down those occasional urges to binge on certain foods.

Too many people get into food ruts. Breakfast has to be bacon, fried eggs, hash browns, toast, and coffee, or it just isn't breakfast. Lunch has to be a ham sandwich and potato chips. Dinner has to be meat, potatoes, and dessert. If this is you, you don't know what you're missing—or what your body is missing. Not only are you missing out on a wonderful array of taste treats and delightful food adventures, but your body is most likely short of vital nutrients. I believe that strictly limited food patterns, together with lack of exercise, are responsible for most of the chronic diseases we find today. A few foods are overrepresented at mealtimes while the body is starving for others.

Let's start thinking in terms of variety. Don't stick to the same ingredients in your salads all the time. Use different kinds of leaf lettuce, not your favorite all the time. Put some raw spinach leaves in, or dandelion greens, or wild miner's lettuce. Put in bits of broccoli and cauliflower as well as the usual celery, onions, and tomatoes. Make hearty vegetable soups with different vegetable combinations. Don't have orange juice every morning—try grape juice, apricot nectar, pineapple juice, or a combination like apple-cherry juice. Use a different salad dressing every day.

Cooking can be fun, and mealtimes can become wonderful adventures. Every food has a unique taste to itself, something to discover and savor. Jump out of the food rut, if you're in one, and learn to have a good time with your meals.

SUPPLEMENTS

It is often helpful to take supplements when following a reducing diet, not only to avoid aggravating previously existing vitamin and mineral deficiencies during the period of lower daily calorie intake, but also to prevent complications from any condition you may have. For the latter reason, it is best to get counseling from a nutritionist before beginning a reducing diet.

Millions of Americans who carry undiagnosed hypertension, Type II diabetes, hypoglycemia, atherosclerosis, hypothyroidism, anemia, and other conditions need qualified professional advice before dieting. Supportive supplements may include a good multiple vitamin-mineral tablet each day, digestive enzyme supplements, natural laxatives, fiber, diuretics, heart support, and glandular system support.

I have sometimes found that overweight patients at the Ranch have an underactive thyroid, and it is very important for such persons to take a thyroid supplement to avoid further glandular imbalances. Check with your doctor first.

Potassium is particularly indicated as a supplement during reducing programs to help protect the heart and to counter the water-retention effect caused by excess sodium. Your doctor will be able to help select the supplements you need.

I always recommend supplements that I know to be of help in reducing. Four alfalfa tablets should be taken at the beginning of each meal, cracked between the teeth and swallowed with water to promote bowel health and cleanliness. Two of my Digest-It enzyme capsules can be taken with each meal to improve digestion and assimilation. One or two beet tablets with each meal will aid liver function and serve as a mild laxative. Wheat bran or psyllium husks add bulk and fiber to the bowel and speed up elimination. A level teaspoonful of psyllium or 2 tablespoons of wheat bran should be taken after each meal.

I recommend a tablespoon of wheat germ oil twice a day, a teaspoon of rice polishings three times daily, and 50 milligrams of niacin after every meal. KB-11 or Cleavers tea, available at most health food stores, can be taken between meals to stimulate the kidneys. If the kidneys become overworked, I advise patients to cut down on fruit and fruit juices, especially citrus. Liquid chlorophyll in a glass of water is a wonderful cleansing drink that has no calories whatsoever. If water retention is a problem for you, use herbal extracts or tablets instead of teas and chlorophyll drinks.

DO YOU KNOW HOW TO EAT?

Everyone knows how to stuff food in his mouth. But I have found many people who do not know how to eat. Does that surprise you? Eating is considered an art in some places, but I am talking about something a little different. For proper digestion and assimilation, we need to know how to eat properly.

These are those who bolt down their food like starving wolves. There are parents who wait until dinnertime to criticize or discipline their children. There are husbands and wives who argue at mealtimes. There are those who read a book or newspaper while they eat, hardly aware of whether they are consuming food or their napkins. And, last but not least, there is the TV dinner crowd. I don't mean those who eat prepackaged TV dinners, but those who sit and eat while absorbed in their favorite soap opera, sports event, or series program. Both reading and TV watching involve the functioning of the nervous system and glands in ways that can interfere with digestion and assimilation.

Keeping at the right weight isn't a matter of always eating the low-calorie foods; it's often a matter of eating only when we are truly hungry. We don't have to eat just to keep our stomachs full. Some people believe that three meals a day are absolutely necessary, and I think in most cases we find out that to miss an occasional meal, or to have a very small meal, could be very good for us.

It is more important to eat only until our hunger is satisfied than to see how much we can eat. When we overeat, we abuse the digestive system. If we don't have enough, we starve. We can starve for a short time and live on accumulated fat, protein, and starch reserves in the body, but we find out there is a limit to our reserves. That's why crash diets or imbalanced diets are not the best for us.

Mealtimes should be special, pleasant occasions when the whole family gets together to do nothing else but eat and enjoy one another's company. Talking is fine, but it must be limited to positive, enjoyable subjects. If a child talks so much that his or her food is getting cold, the parents, of course, should lovingly insist that the child eat and save some of the conversation for later.

Pay attention to the food, right from the start. Compliment "the cook" often for his or her work and artful preparation.

Notice dishes that look especially attractive or that have a wonderful smell, and remark about them out loud. When you try your first few bites, tell the others how good you think the food is. Look at what you are eating; notice the color, texture, and savory scent of it; savor it in your mouth. Chew well and slowly. If you are in the habit of rushing, put your fork down between bites until each mouthful is thoroughly chewed.

If you are "the cook," I want to encourage you to make the food served look nice as well as taste nice. Beauty is a wonderful aid to the digestion. When you come to the table yourself after preparing a lovely meal, don't hesitate to say things like, "Doesn't this look nice?" or "M-m-m-m, everything smells wonderful!" Feel free to do this whether anyone else says anything or not. Cooking is a special art and skill, and you have every right to feel proud of your cooking—and to enjoy it with relish.

I make these suggestions not to encourage meaningless rituals but to stir the digestive juices, to stimulate the brain and nerves to prepare the digestive system to function efficiently. When we both enjoy and pay attention to our food as we eat, I believe digestion and assimilation are more efficient. We get more nourishment from our food—and there is less chance of overeating. When we eat too fast, our brains don't get the signal to stop eating until we have overeaten, and this is a common experience for many chronically overweight persons.

Reading or watching TV at mealtimes reduces stimulation of the gastric juices and sometimes places the glandular system in opposition to the digestive system. If what you are reading or watching is exciting, adrenaline is released from the adrenal glands, which causes constriction of the blood vessels to the stomach and bowel, hindering digestion and assimilation. My advice is, *don't do it.* You're wasting food and your money and putting a strain on your digestive system.

It is especially important for those watching their weight to never eat a heavy meal later than two hours before bedtime.

COOKING TIPS TO GET MORE FOR YOUR MONEY

One of the most frequent wastes of food budget money and nutrients is to overcook food, destroying vitamins, enzymes, and minerals. A friend of mine who visited South Africa commented on the high incidence of hardening of the arteries and relatively poor health among urbanized natives. Blacks who live in the rural villages of South Africa are often very healthy on a food regimen high in whole grain cereals and vegetables, with a little meat now and then. But when they move to the cities, many subsist on a sort of stew made by boiling water, vegetables, meat, and as much as a handful of salt together. After the solids are eaten, the leftover liquid is thrown away, along with whatever vitamins and minerals have not been destroyed by the prolonged cooking or exposure to air during cooking. *This is a disease diet, for the body can't long subsist on overcooked, depleted, devitaminized foods.*

The best way to cook almost anything is at low heat until just barely done. For fruit, this means when it is soft. Vegetables should still have an edge of crispness to them and possibly be a little underdone. Meat should be baked or roasted in the oven at low heat over as long a period of time as possible without undue inconvenience. There are many recent cookbooks that give instructions for doing this. Most juices and flavors are retained.

I believe the best way to cook vegetables is in low-heat, waterless, stainless steel cookware. Second best is steaming them. Many stores now carry stainless steel steamer inserts, short-legged, round, folding-leaf devices that fit inside pots to keep vegetables, grains, or other foods above the water as they cook in the steam. Electric Crock-Pots are all right, and using a pressure cooker now and then is acceptable. However, I do not believe microwave oven cooking is necessarily wise, because we don't fully understand what effects can come from using intense radiation to cook foods.

When you go to the supermarket, you usually try to make the most of your food dollars. Don't throw them away later by overcooking.

A good tip: Save the vegetable water when you steam vegetables and use it to make soups or to cook whole grain cereals. That cooking water has good vitamins, minerals, and flavor in it, and adds to the taste of anything you use it with.

GETTING DOWN TO BUSINESS

Now it is time to talk business about starting your diet. We find that it is always best to think and plan ahead, to make sure everything goes smoothly.

Your family members can eat everything you will be eating, the only difference being that they will be able to eat more of some things than you are allowing yourself. If my diet is extremely different from your former family food pattern, you may have to ease them into it. For example, if they are used to eating a good deal of pork and beef, gradually cut down on the number of times per week they are served. Use more chicken and fish. Encourage them to eat more vegetables and avoid fatty foods (see Table 9.5). Their health and vitality will improve, sometimes dramatically.

One of the most effective ways to lose weight by dieting is to "pair up" with at least one other friend and do it together. If your spouse needs to diet and is willing, that will be a big boost to both of you. Resolve in advance to encourage and compliment one another on looks and progress. Go shopping together and buy yourself outfits in a smaller size than you wear now. Then, hang them up someplace in the house where you will see them often.

When going out to dinner, either at a friend's house or at a restaurant, eat a salad first at home to reduce any temptation to eat excessively or to make wrong food choices. It's much easier to avoid making inappropriate food choices once you've taken the edge off your appetite.

Remember, too, that a half hour of active exercise each day, to the point of perspiring and breathing heavily, will raise your metabolic level for hours longer, helping burn off fat calories long after you have stopped exercising.

Think positively about yourself and your diet. Think positively about getting off the diet and onto a healthy way of living and eating, as described in chapter 4. Use your head to get ahead.

Study my food charts and diet plan. Vegetarians can substitute dairy products, tofu, grains, legumes, nut and seed butters, and eggs for meat. Nonvegetarians and vegetarians alike can make alterations as desired in meal composition, as long as the basic plan is followed. My food charts make it easy for you to rearrange any meal to suit your taste.

Water, herb tea, coffee substitutes, broth, or vegetable juice may be taken between meals, *always at least an hour and a half before the next meal.*

Use a variety of salad dressings. I don't believe in using much oil on salads since we get enough in other foods. You are allowed to use blue cheese, roquefort, vinegar and oil, yogurt, avocado dressing, oil with lemon and honey, and similar dressings.

SPECIAL NOTES ABOUT SALADS

Salads are a key factor in any good weight-loss diet program, and it is possible to be very creative with them. A high-fiber diet helps drive excess cholesterol out of the system, tones the bowel, and ensures regularity. Best vegetables for salads are the leaf lettuces (head lettuce is almost nutritionally worthless), spinach leaves, watercress, parsley, celery, cucumbers, tomatoes, alfalfa sprouts (and other sprouts), onions, garlic, and grated raw vegetables, such as carrots, beets, parsnips, zucchini, turnips, and so on (only use a little of each grated vegetable per salad and use two or three). Some can't take the onions or garlic, or they live or work with people who can't take the odors, so use them with discretion.

There are many other things we can use in salads, such as avocado, sliced mushrooms, sliced raw green beans, raw pieces of cauliflower and broccoli, sliced bell peppers, chives, fresh coriander, herbs of various kinds such as anise, chard, miner's lettuce, and raw beet, mustard, dandelion, and turnip greens (these can become tough, so test first). Some things I don't believe in are croutons, bacon bits, and other embellishments that usually come from packages.

It is a wonderful idea to mix or sprinkle wheat germ, which is high in magnesium, a little dulse flakes, grated cheddar or parmesan cheese, ground nuts, or seeds into salads.

Table 9.5. Fatty Foods to Use Sparingly or to Avoid

Food	Total Fat%	Saturated Fatty Acids %	Cholesterol (mg/100 gm)
Lard	100	38	95
Oils:			
cottonseed	100	25	0
corn	100	10	0
olive	100	11	0
safflower	100	8	0
sesame	100	15	0
sunflower seed	100	12	0
Butter	81	46	250
Margarine	81	18	N/A
Pecans (raw)	71	5	0
Brazil nuts (raw)	67	13	0
Walnuts (raw)	64	4	0
Coconut (dried)	63	54	0
Hazelnuts (raw)	62	3	0
Bacon, fried	59	19	N/A
Almonds (raw)	54	4	0
Pistachios (raw)	54	3	0
Eggs, yolk only	31	10	1,500
whole	12	4	550
Liver, average	4	2	300
Pork chops, broiled	38	14	70
Lamb chops, broiled	31	17	70
Veal chops, broiled	11	6	90
Cheese: Cheddar	33	18	100
Cream	32	18	120

EXTREME DIETS

In extreme cases, I have used a special diet that is more effective in bringing weight loss, but it should only be used in consultation with or under supervision from a doctor. There are some persons who find it very difficult to lose weight on even a properly balanced reducing diet, and I have made a special effort to help them.

Some researchers have called the left side of the body the negative side and the right side, the positive side. Foods that feed the left side are called negative foods, such as potatoes, cereal grains, starches, sweet fruits, and so forth; foods that feed the right side are called positive foods, such as meat, fish, eggs, cheese, milk, and so forth. Vegetables are neutral and can be used on both diets. I never recommend citrus fruit for heart patients.

The following is a right side or positive diet and should only be used for three days to one week at a time; *it should never be used by those with heart problems.* Most overweight people have taken too much of the starchy foods (I believe that people with heart disease need complex carbohydrates and starches in their daily food intake) in the past and that's why we give the more positive diet, to restore balance. Then we are ready to go on with my regular Health and Harmony Food Regimen. Understand that these extreme diets are only to be used for a limited time when a body is obese due to chemical imbalance. The following is an extreme positive diet and is only for balancing the body, which is already in an extreme imbalanced direction.

Two or three meals per day should each include:
Lean meat or fish

Sliced fresh tomatoes
One or two vegetables

Fruit with cottage cheese may be taken for breakfast. This diet burns fat rapidly but may cause heart palpitations, chest pains, and other symptoms because this positive diet does not support the heart properly, which is on the left or negative side of the body.

In other cases, with people who had become overweight due to an extreme positive diet, I have used an extreme negative diet made up of:

Sweet fruits
Rice as a cereal and other starches
Low-calorie vegetables

This diet, too, must only be used under a doctor's supervision because it is considered an extreme negative diet. This will support the heart well in many cases, but it is not a balanced diet. When this diet is over, it is best to start my Health and Harmony Food Regimen.

LOWEST-CALORIE VEGETABLES

The lowest-calorie vegetable dish is a mixed green salad, two cups of which come to 50 calories or less. There are more than 50 calories in a tablespoon of dressing, so be conservative with the dressing. The following vegetables are cooked unless noted as raw; also see Table 9.6 later in the chapter. You can eat as much of these as you wish, especially the salad vegetables.

Table 9.6. **Vegetables Lowest in Calories**		
Food	*Amount*	*Calories*
Fresh green string beans	½ cup	15
Beet greens	½ cup	9
Broccoli,	½ cup	20
raw	½ cup	27
Cabbage, raw	½ cup	12
Carrots	½ cup	24
Cauliflower,	½ cup	10
raw	½ cup	15
Celery,	½ cup	8
raw	½ cup	6
Cucumber	10 slices	10
Garlic	1 clove	6
Eggplant	½ cup	17
Kale	½ cup	16
Leaf lettuce	1 cup	16
Okra	½ cup	11
Parsley	½ cup	13
Green peppers, raw	1 medium	10
Radishes, raw	1 radish	1
Summer squash	½ cup	12–17

TWO THIRTY-DAY DIET PLANS

The two thirty-day diet plans presented on the following pages are designed for you to create meals from calorie charts of the various food groups and foods I recommend. Meal planning and food selection are left up to you, so you can design meals uniquely suited to you (and your family members, if you choose to include them). You may continue this diet for thirty days or as much longer as you desire, based on how you feel in body and mind. Consult your doctor if you feel that you need professional advice.

1,200 Calories/Day Diet Plan

Our basic goal with breakfast is two fruits (or one fruit and one fruit juice) and one different cereal grain (no wheat) each day for three to five days before having the same one again. If you select two fruits, have a cup of broth, herb tea, or chlorophyll and water half an hour before breakfast. Count calories before preparing the meal, staying as close as possible to 300. (If you plan to have a Waldorf salad, gelatin with fruit, or mixed fruit salad for lunch, skip the breakfast fruit and add a selection from the crackers and bread group [Table 9.8] or raw nuts and seeds group [Table 9.15].)

Breakfast Option A
(300 Calories)
1 selection from the drink group (Table 9.10)
1 or 2 selections from the fruit group (Table 9.12)
1 selection from column 2 of the dairy group (Table 9.9)
or 2 selections from column 1

Breakfast Option B
(300 Calories)
1 selection from the drink group (Table 9.10)
1 or 2 selections from the fruit group (Table 9.12)
1 selection from column 2 of the cereal grain group
(no wheat; Table 9.7)
1 selection from column 2 of the natural sweeteners group
(Table 9.14)

Notice that my food tables are varied enough not to select too many calories or too few. If you are under 300 calories, fill in by adding a Ry-Krisp cracker or sprinkle a teaspoon of ground-up nuts or seeds on something you're eating.

Snack: 10 A.M.
(70 to 80 Calories)
Select one or more items from the snack group (Table 9.18).

If you choose 80 calories in morning snacks, I suggest that you limit yourself to 60 or 70 calories in the afternoon.

Our basic goal with lunch is to have one high-calorie starch or two starches (one high calorie, such as a baked potato, and one low calorie, such as millet or zucchini). But if you had a column 2 helping of a whole grain cereal (no wheat) for breakfast, you should have a protein at this meal. If you did not have fruit or fruit juice for breakfast, have a fruit salad for lunch.

Lunch Option A
(400 Calories)
1 selection from the soup group (Table 9.19)
1 selection from the salad group (Table 9.16)
1 selection from the salad dressings group
(2 tablespoons; Table 9.17)
1 selection from the crackers and bread group
(no wheat; Table 9.8)
1 selection from column 2 of the cereal grain and
starch group (Table 9.7)
or
1 selection from the dairy group (Table 9.9)
3 selections from the vegetable group (Table 9.20)

Lunch Option B
(400 Calories)
1 selection from the salad group (Table 9.16)
1 selection from column 2 of the cereal grain and starch
group (no wheat; Table 9.7)
or
1 selection from the dairy group (Table 9.9)
3 or more selections from the vegetable group (Table 9.20)

You may use a little butter or margarine on your vegetables and, if you must have salt, use a little sea salt. Be sure to try one or more of the vegetable seasonings or broth powders available at your local health food store. They taste salty and add much more flavor than salt. You would be doing a favor to your body by switching from salt to a vegetable seasoning.

Snack: 3 P.M.
(60 to 80 Calories)
Select one or more items from the snack group (Table 9.18)

If you had an 80-calorie snack in the morning, don't go over 70 calories now. Save 50 calories for your evening snack.

For the dinner meal, we always have a large vegetable salad and at least two cooked vegetables. Because many people prefer to have their main meat dish at this meal, I have put it here, but it is just as valid to have it at the lunch meal and have the main starch of the day at dinner. You can do this if you wish. Limit meat to one or at most two meals per week. Have fish or poultry at other times. An omelet or serving of cottage cheese occasionally is permitted.

Dinner Option A

(300 Calories)

Large salad of mixed raw vegetables

1 selection from the meat, poultry, and fish group

(Table 9.13)

3 or more selections from the vegetable group (Table 9.20),
including 1 summer or winter squash

There is no second option for dinner, except the switching of the main starch to this meal.

After-Dinner Snack

(50 Calories)

Select one or more items from the snack group

(Table 9.18)

1,800 Calories/Day Diet Plan

The strategies for breakfast, lunch, and dinner are no different on this diet as compared to the 1,200 Calories/Day Diet Plan. The key is still to use whole cereal grains (no wheat), two fresh fruits daily, at least six vegetables, one starch, and one protein. Keep in mind that 50 to 60 percent of the fruit and vegetables should be raw. Try to have a large mixed vegetable salad twice a day most days, and use the other salads for an occasional break in your routine. I advise fruit salad no more than once a week. Use dried fruit sparingly (Table 9.11). Remember, vegetables taste wonderful seasoned with some of the natural salt-free seasonings found in health food stores. There is no reason for your meals to be bland in taste. Learn to use herbal seasonings. Add up calories before preparing meals.

Breakfast

(450 Calories)

1 selection from the drink group (Table 9.10)

½ hour before eating

(take 1 fruit juice)

1 selection from column 2 of the dairy group

(Table 9.9),

or 2 selections from column 1

1 selection from column 1 of the cereal grain and

starch group (no wheat; Table 9.7)

2 selections from the fruit group (Table 9.12)

1 selection from the natural sweeteners group

(Table 9.14)

Snack: 10 A.M.

(100 Calories)

Select one or more items from the snack group

(Table 9.18)

Lunch

(600 Calories)

1 selection from the soup group

(80 calories or more; Table 9.19)

1 selection from the salad group (Table 9.16)

1 selection from the salad dressing group

(double portion okay; Table 9.17)

1 selection from column 1 of the raw nuts and seeds group

(add to salad; Table 9.15)

1 selection from column 2 of the cereal grain and starch

group (no wheat; Table 9.7)

1 selection from the crackers and bread group

(no wheat; Table 9.8)

Snack: 3 P.M.

(100 Calories)

Select one or more items from the snack group (Table 9.18)

Dinner

(450 Calories)

1 selection from column 2 of the meat, poultry, and fish
group (Table 9.13)

1 large mixed vegetable salad with double dressing

4 selections from the vegetable group (Table 9.20), including
1 cooked green vegetable,

1 root vegetable, 1 yellow vegetable, and 1 squash in season

1 selection from the crackers and bread group (no wheat;
Table 9.8), butter allowed

After-Dinner Snack

(100 Calories)

Select one or more items from the snack group (Table 9.18)

NUTS AND SEEDS

You can purchase raw nut and seed butters at most health food
stores or if you have a Champion juicer, you can make them
yourself. They make wonderful snack spreads, salad dressings
(diluted), and blender drinks with milk, apple juice, pineapple
juice, carrot juice, or herbal teas.

Alternately, you can grind up nuts and seeds finely in a
blender to sprinkle on salads, cooked vegetables, whole grain
cereals, soups, and other dishes to add nutritional value. Nuts
and seeds are high in calcium, phosphorus, iron, and potassium
and have a sprinkling of the B vitamins. We get our finest oils
from seeds and nuts for building the nerves, glands, and brain.
There is no cholesterol in the oils found in nuts and seeds.

Table 9.7. **Cereal Grain and Starch Group**

Food (Cooked)	Column 1 Amount	Calories	Column 2 Amount	Calories
Whole or cracked wheat	⅓ cup	70	—	—
Buckwheat groats★	⅓ cup	60	—	—
Brown rice	⅓ cup	60	⅔ cup	120
Rolled or steel-cut oats	½ cup	65	—	—
Pearled barley	¼ cup	72	½ cup	144
Whole or cracked rye	¼ cup	67	—	—
Millet★	½ cup	87	¾ cup	130
Yellow cornmeal★★	½ cup	58	—	—
Yellow corn grits★★	½ cup	62	—	—
Cornbread	1 ounce	55	—	—
Sweet potato★★★	—	—	1 med. (4 oz.)	154
Yam★★★	—	—	1 med. (5 oz.)	155
Baked potato★★★	—	—	1 med. (4 oz.)	102
Lentils	—	—	1 cup	122

★Prepare millet and buckwheat by allowing 3 parts water to 1 part grain; soak overnight in boiling water in wide-mouth thermos. Other grains allow 2 to 1.

★★Always stir cornmeal or corn grits into cold water and bring to boil before allowing to sit, to avoid lumping.

★★★Yams, sweet potatoes, and potatoes can be baked in the oven wrapped in foil to preserve moisture.

Table 9.8. **Crackers and Bread Group**

Food	Amount	Calories
Ry-Krisp	2	60
Sesame	6	60
Ak-Mak	4	60
Rye bread	1 slice	56
Cracked wheat	1 slice	60
Whole wheat	1 slice	55

Table 9.9. **Dairy Group**

Food/Drink	Column 1		Column 2	
	Amount	Calories	Amount	Calories
Nonfat milk	1 cup	90	2 cups	180
Raw whole cow milk	½ cup	80	1 cup	160
Raw whole goat milk	½ cup	82	1 cup	164
Yogurt, plain	½ cup	80	1 cup	160
Low-fat cottage cheese	⅔ cup	80	1⅓ cup	160
Egg, poached or boiled	1	80	2	160
Cream cheese	1½ table-spoons	80	3 table-spoons	160
Blue or roquefort cheese	1½ table-spoons	80	3 table-spoons	160
Cheddar cheese	1 ounce	112	1½ ounce	168
Swiss cheese	1 ounce	104	1½ ounce	156
Tofu	⅔ cup	80	1⅓ cup	160
Ricotta cheese	2 ounce	60	4 ounce	120

Table 9.10. Drink Group

Drink	Amount	Calories
Apple juice	4 ounce (½ cup)	63
Apricot nectar	4 ounce	70
Grape juice	4 ounce	80
Pineapple juice	4 ounce	60
Prune juice	4 ounce	85
Strawberry juice	4 ounce	52
Cherry concentrate	1 tsp. in 8 ouncewater	19
Vegetable broth	1 tsp. in 8 ouncewater	3
Chlorophyll drink	1 tsp. in 8 ouncewater	0
Lemongrass tea	8 ounce	0
Comfrey tea	8 ounce	0
Peppermint tea	8 ounce	0
Shavegrass tea	8 ounce	0
Spearmint tea	8 ounce	0
Coffee substitute	8 ounce	2

Note: Juices may be mixed half and half with cold herb teas to reduce the calorie intake or to extend the quantity while holding the calories constant.

Table 9.11. Dried Fruit Group

Food	Calories (3½-ounce serving)	Food	Calories (3½-ounce serving)
Apples	289	Figs	270
Apricots	265	Pears	270
Banana	340	Peaches	263
Currants	273	Prunes	255
Dates	274	Raisins	279

Note: Dried fruits have more concentrated fruit sugars than fresh fruit because it has less water. Use them sparingly to sweeten other foods or reconstitute winter fruits by soaking them in boiling water.

Table 9.12. **Fresh Fruit Group**

Food	Amount	Calories
Apple	1 large	120
Apricots	2 medium	54
Avocado	1 large	360
Banana	1 medium	128
Blackberries	1 cup	46
Blueberries	1 cup	96
Cantaloupe	½ medium	40
Cherries	1½ dozen	67
Cranberries	1 cup	48
Currants:		
red	½ cup	24
black	½ cup	30
Figs	1 medium	30
Grapefruit	½ medium	54
Grapes	1 cup	104
Guava (peeled)	1 medium	56
Honeydew melon	⅙ large	68
Loganberries	1 cup	64
Loquats	3½ ounces	56
Lychees	3½ ounces	64
Mango	½ medium	69
Muskmelon	½ medium	52
Nectarines	1 medium	50
Orange	1 medium	88
Papaya	1 large	160
Passion fruit	3½ ounces	91
Peaches	1 medium	43
Pears	1 medium	111
Persimmons	1 medium	96
Pineapple	1 cup	73
Plums	2 medium	60
Prunes (cooked)	1 medium	43

Quince (cooked)	1 medium	51
Raspberries:		
red	1 cup	76
black	1 cup	91
Rhubarb (cooked)	½ cup	190
Strawberries	1 cup	55
Tangerines	1 large	52
Watermelon	8 ounce slice	120

Note: You may want to use fruits as desserts or to sweeten other foods, such as cereal grains or plain yogurt. Use sun-ripened fruits where possible and avoid unripe fruits or fruits picked green for shipping to market. Fruits have more vitamins, vegetables have more minerals, generally speaking.

Table 9.13. **Meat, Poultry, and Fish Group**

Food	Column 1		Column 2	
	Amount	Calories	Amount	Calories
Lean beef	2 oz.	140	3 oz.	210
Calf liver	2 oz.	135	3 oz.	197
Veal cutlet	2 oz.	127	3 oz.	191
Lamb chop, lean	2 oz.	132	3 oz.	198
Leg of lamb	2 oz.	106	4 oz.	212
Chicken	3 oz.	115	5 oz.	190
Game hen	3 oz.	120	5 oz.	200
Turkey	2 oz.	146	3 oz.	213
Salmon	3 oz.	147	4 oz.	196
Trout	4 oz.	108	8 oz.	216
Shad	2 oz.	110	4 oz.	220
Tuna	2 oz.	107	4 oz.	214
Swordfish	3 oz.	144	4 oz.	184
Cod	6 oz.	120	10 oz.	200
Halibut	4 oz.	137	6 oz.	204
Flounder	2 oz.	112	4 oz.	224

Table 9.14. **Natural Sweeteners Group★**

Food	Column 1 Calories/ Tablespoon	Column 2 Calories/ Teaspoon
Maple syrup	64	21
Honey	80	27
Molasses	67	22
Carob powder	18	6
Apple concentrate	60	20
Cherry concentrate	56	19
Grape concentrate	72	24
Dates, dried, chopped	46	15
Figs, dried, chopped	42	14
Prunes	44	15
Raisins	44	15
Apricots, dried	39	13
Pears, dried	19	6

★Be very sparing in your use of these concentrated sweeteners.

Table 9.15. **Raw Nuts and Seeds Group (Butters and Fine Grinds)**

Food	Column 1 Calories/ Tablespoon	Column 2 Calories/ Teaspoon
Almonds	90	30
Cashews	85	28
Pecans	103	34
Hazelnuts	98	33
Walnuts	98	33
Sesame seeds	22	7
Sunflower seeds	84	28
Pumpkin seeds (pepitas)	83	28

Table 9.16. Salad Group

Food	Amount	Calories
Mixed vegetables (6–8)★	2 cups	50
Coleslaw (with dressing)	1 cup	151
Carrot/raisin	1 cup	204
Cucumber/yogurt dressing	1 cup	90
Gelatin with fruit	6 ounce	120
Gelatin with vegetables	6 ounce	110
Waldorf salad	6 ounce	170
Mixed fruit	6 ounce	170

★ Romaine, red leaf lettuce, butter lettuce, celery, radishes, cucumber, tomato, parsley, green onions, green bell pepper, watercress, endive, broccoli bits, and cauliflower bits. Grate raw carrot, beet, turnip, and/or parsnip on top to make it a rainbow salad.

Table 9.17. Salad Dressings Group

Food	Amount	Calories
Blue cheese	1 tablespoon	76
French	1 tablespoon	62
Thousand Island	1 tablespoon	75
Vinegar and oil	1 tablespoon	83
Avocado	⅙ large	62
Roquefort	1 tablespoon	76
Italian	1 tablespoon	83
Mayonnaise	1 tablespoon	110
Lemon juice and oil	1 tablespoon	83
Herb, oil, and vinegar★	1 tablespoon	83

★Herb, oil, and vinegar dressing is made by using 3 parts cold pressed vegetable oil to 1 part wine vinegar, then adding any mixture of garlic, parsley, fresh oregano, dill, sweet basil, thyme, and grated lemon peel. Allow to age from 1 to 2 weeks.

SNACKS

You can arrange your snacks and snacktimes any way you wish, picking any combination from the list that adds up to the allowable snack calories per day. Combinations such as nut butter and cheese, nut butter or cream cheese and celery, crackers and nut butter or cheese all make satisfying snacks. Simply cut down the amount of each to fit the calorie requirement as necessary for a particular snacktime. Use lettuce or zucchini instead of bread, and put snack fillers on them for a treat. I am not encouraging snacks, but allowing them for those who have to have something extra. If you don't feel like having a snack, don't have one. You can skip the morning snack and double up on the afternoon snack or vice versa, but I recommend against doing that with the evening snack. Evening snacks are more likely to turn to fat than any others. For that reason, I strongly recommend that you stick to such snacks as vegetables, broth, crackers, and herb tea after dinner.

Table 9.18. **Snack Group**

Fruit	Calories
Banana, small	80
Orange, sections	80
Apple, ½	60
Fig, small fresh	30
Fig, large dried	60
Cantaloupe, ½	60
Honeydew, slice (10 ounce)	70
Watermelon, slice (10 ounce)	75
Pear, ½ large	70
Prunes, 3 stewed	75

Pineapple, raw cubes, 1 cup	75
Peach, large	50
Cherries, 20	75
Mango, half, 4 ounce	70
Papaya, 7 ounce	75
Guava, 4 ounce	60
Strawberries, 1 cup	60
Plum, medium	30
Dates, dried, each	10
Olives, ripe, each	13
Avocado, ⅙ large	62

Drinks

Herb tea	0
Broth, 1 cup	30
w/1 tablespoon lecithin granules	80
Coffee substitute	0
Carrot juice, 8 ounce	50

Vegetables

Carrot, medium	30
Tomato, medium sliced	35
Celery, large stalk	5
Broccoli, 3 ounce	30
Cucumber slices, each	1
Radishes, each	2
Sprouts, 1 cup	16

Nuts (Raw)

Almonds, each	7
Cashews, each	8.5
Pecans, each	5
Walnuts, each	8
Sunflower seeds, 2 tablespoons	70

(Continued)

Table 9.18. **Continued**

Crackers	Calories
Ry–Krisp, 2	60
Sesame, 6	60
Ak–Mak, 4 squares	60
Cheese	
Cheddar, ½ slice (½ ounce)	56
Cream, 1 tablespoon	53
Cottage, ½ cup	60
Swiss, ½ slice (½ ounce)	52
Nut and Seed Butters	
Almond	52
Cashew	35
Pumpkin seed	34
Sesame	19
Sunflower	35
Walnut	41
Other	
Yogurt, ⅓ cup	53

Table 9.19. **Soup Group**

Food	Amount	Calories
Beef broth	1 cup	30
Vegetable broth	1 cup	5
Chicken broth	1 cup	22
Split pea	1 cup	148
Vegetable soup	1 cup	80
Onion soup	1 cup	90
Lentil soup	1 cup	130

Note: To make a nice protein broth, add nut butter or tofu to broth. You can also add egg yolk, as the Chinese do.

∽ Best Three Reducing Foods in Each Chart

Cereal Grains	Calories/100 grams or 3½ ounces
Brown rice	87
Rye	81
Millet	78

Fruits (raw)	
Cantaloupe	25
Watermelon	27
Strawberries	37

Soups	Calories per Cup
Vegetable broth	5
Chicken broth	22
Vegetable soup	80

Snacks	
Ry-Krisp (2)	60
Chico-San rice crackers	70
Sesame seed butter (1 tablespoon)	82

Natural Sweeteners	
Honey	305
Carob powder	18
Raisins	44

Proteins (broiled)	
Halibut	130
Salmon (baked)	182
Chicken, roasted	199

Vegetables (raw)	
Celery	13
Radish	17
Leaf lettuce (sprouts, watercress)	17

(Continued)

Vegetables (cooked)	Calories/100 grams or 3½ ounces
Zucchini (steamed)	14
Broccoli	26
Green beans	35
Beets	31
Carrots	45

Drinks	
1 teaspoon chlorophyll in cup of hot water	0
Herbal teas	0
Carrot juice (8 oz.)	97

Seasonings	
Vegetable broth powder (instead of salt)	6 per 1 gram
Cayenne pepper (instead of black pepper)	less than 1 per 1 gram
Sweet basil	4 per 1 gram

Table 9.20. **Vegetable Group**

Food (Cooked except as noted)	Amount	Calories
Artichoke	1 small	50
Asparagus	8 stalks	32
Beans, fresh	½ cup	15
Beans, lima	½ cup	80
Beets	½ cup	30
Beets, raw	1 tablespoon	5
Beet greens	½ cup	9
Broccoli	½ cup	20
Broccoli, raw	½ cup	27
Brussels sprouts	20	20
Cabbage, steamed	½ cup	34

Cabbage, raw	½ cup	12
Carrots	½ cup	24
Carrots, raw	½ cup	62
Carrot, raw	1 medium	30
Cauliflower	½ cup	10
Cauliflower, raw	½ cup	15
Celery	½ cup	8
Celery, raw	½ cup	6
Chives	1 tablespoon	3
Cob corn	½ ear	70
Corn kernels	½ cup	85
Cucumber	10 slices	10
Garlic	1 clove	6
Eggplant	½ cup	17
Kale	½ cup	16
Leaf lettuce	2 leaves	8
Leaf lettuce, raw	1 cup	16
Okra	½ cup	11
Onions, green, raw	6 each	20
Onions, mature	½ cup	25
Parsley, raw	½ cup	13
Parsnips	½ cup	53
Peas, fresh or frozen	½ cup	35
Pepper, green, raw	1 medium	10
Radishes, raw	6 each	6
Spinach, raw or cooked	½ cup	20
Squash:		
Summer	½ cup	15
Winter	½ cup	39
Zucchini	½ cup	12
Zucchini, raw	½ cup	17
Butternut	½ cup	25
Tomatoes	½ cup	25
Tomatoes, raw	1 medium	35

Note: These amounts make small portions, which are adequate if you use enough variety. Variety is necessary to provide the body with all the chemical elements it needs.

MY SPECIAL TWO-WEEK DIET

This reducing diet is for two weeks. You are to have no dried or stewed fruit; have only fresh fruits. No pies, cakes, cookies, breads, ice cream, or pastries of any kind are allowed.

Allowed Seasonings: Use herbs or broth seasoning. No salt.

Breads: Chico-San rice cakes (unsalted), Ry-Krisp (unsalted), Finn Crisp (rye), Wasa (light rye).

Vegetable Broth: Potato peeling broth, vegetable broth. Broth seasoning can be made into a vegetable drink.

Desserts: Gelatin made with apple, cherry, or grape concentrates or pineapple juice (with no added sugar). You may have this three times a week only.

Dressings: Tomato juice and avocado. Apple cider vinegar with 1 teaspoon sesame seed oil or honey. Apple cider vinegar, avocado, and broth seasoning.

Fats: Butter, one teaspoon daily.

Beverages: Herb tea, vegetable broth, potato peeling broth, vegetable juices (fresh only), cereal coffee substitute—no sugar or cream.

To control appetite: One tablespoon whey in a vegetable drink or broth, fifteen minutes before each meal.

Meal Suggestions

Breakfast: Fresh fruit, protein, health drink.

Lunch: Vegetable salad (five or six vegetables), avocado every other day, health drink.

Dinner: Small salad, two cooked vegetables, protein, health drink.

Food Selections

Fruit (must be fresh—no dried fruits allowed)
Berries

Melons

Cherries

Grapes

Apples

Banana (1 per day)

Papaya

Peaches

Pears

Apricots

Plums

Pineapple

Orange or grapefruit (sections only)

Nectarines

Vegetables for lunch salad
Parsley

Alfalfa sprouts

Celery

Tomatoes

Radishes

Cucumber

Avocado

Shredded beets (raw, the size of a golf ball, every day in your
    salads)

Carrots

Zucchini

Leaf lettuce (no head lettuce)

Endive

Watercress

Cooked vegetables (steamed)

Fresh corn only

Spinach

Mushrooms

Yellow squash

Summer squash

Snow peas

Brussels sprouts

Turnips

Parsnips

Carrots

Banana squash

Beets

Okra

Celery

Tomatoes

Cabbage

String beans

Cauliflower

Broccoli

Asparagus

Onions

Proteins

Meat (three times a week only): bake, broil, or roast

Lean meat (no fat, no pork, no sausage)

Chicken or turkey (no skin)

Lamb

White fish or salmon

Tofu

Sesame seed butter

Cottage cheese

Yogurt

Special Supplements with Each Meal

4 alfalfa tablets (crack before swallowing)

2 Digestaids

1 KB-11 herb tablet or tea

1 dulse tablet (have seaweed or a form of it every day)

SUGGESTED MENUS

Day 1

Breakfast

Nectarine—Peach—Apricots

One or two soft-boiled eggs

Cleaver tea

Lunch

Vegetable salad (five or six vegetables, with color and variety)

Cooked brown rice

Alfalfa tea

Dinner

Small salad

Steamed asparagus and cauliflower

Broiled salmon

Papaya tea

Day 2

Breakfast

Pears

Two-egg omelet

Uva ursi tea

Lunch

Vegetable salad

Cooked millet

Mint tea

Dinner

Small salad

Corn on the cob

Sliced tomatoes

Cottage cheese

Oat straw tea

Gelatin dessert

Day 3

Breakfast

Orange, sections only

Sesame seed butter, 1 tablespoon

Ry-Krisp or Chico-San

Shavegrass tea

Lunch

Vegetable salad

Cooked rye

Papaya tea

Dinner

Small salad

Steamed snow peas with mushrooms

Baked chicken breast, no skin

Alfalfa tea

Day 4

Breakfast

Grapes

One or two poached eggs

Alfalfa tea

Lunch

Vegetable salad

Cooked yellow cornmeal

Shavegrass tea

Dinner

Small salad

Steamed summer squash

Steamed spinach with tofu

Uva ursi tea

Gelatin dessert

Sesame seed butter

Ry-Krisp or Chico-San

Oat straw tea

Day 5

Breakfast

Banana

Cottage cheese

Papaya tea

Lunch

Vegetable salad

Cooked brown rice

Cleaver tea

Dinner

Small salad

Steamed cabbage

Steamed carrots

Day 6

Breakfast

Apple

One- or two-egg omelet

Oat straw tea

Lunch
Vegetable salad
Cooked millet
Uva ursi tea
Dinner
Small salad
Steamed okra
Steamed beets
Broiled lamb chop
Papaya tea
Gelatin dessert

Day 7
Breakfast
Grapefruit, sections only
Plain yogurt
Lemongrass tea
Lunch
Vegetable salad
Cooked rye
Alfalfa tea
Dinner
Small salad
Steamed green beans
Steamed summer squash
Cottage cheese
Mint tea

Day 8
Breakfast
Cherries
Cottage cheese
Mint tea

Lunch
Vegetable salad
Cooked brown rice
Oat straw tea
Dinner
Small salad
Corn on the cob
Steamed asparagus
Sesame seed butter
Shavegrass tea
Gelatin dessert

Day 9
Breakfast
Peach
One or two soft-boiled eggs
Cleaver tea
Lunch
Vegetable salad
Baked banana squash
Lemongrass tea
Dinner
Small salad
Steamed parsnips
Steamed broccoli
Baked sea bass
Alfalfa tea

Day 10
Breakfast
Banana
One or two poached eggs
Uva ursi tea

Lunch

Vegetable salad

Cooked rye

Cleaver tea

Dinner

Small salad

Steamed brussels sprouts

Steamed carrots and celery

Cottage cheese

Oat straw tea

Day 11

Breakfast

Strawberries

Yogurt

Cleaver tea

Lunch

Vegetable salad

Cooked millet

Mint tea

Dinner

Small salad

Steamed spinach and onions

Broiled lean steak

Papaya tea

Day 12

Breakfast

Pears

Plain yogurt

Alfa-mint tea

Lunch

Vegetable salad

Cooked yellow cornmeal

KB-11 herb tea

Dinner

Small salad

Steamed parsnips

Steamed snow peas

Tofu

Cleaver tea

Gelatin dessert

Day 13

Breakfast

Orange sections

Cottage cheese

Oat straw tea

Lunch

Vegetable salad

Cooked brown rice

Shavegrass tea

Dinner

Small salad

Steamed beets

Steamed cauliflower

Baked turkey, no skin

Mint tea

Day 14

Breakfast

Apricots

One- or two-egg omelet

Lemongrass tea

Lunch

Vegetable salad

Cooked millet

Alfalfa tea

Dinner

Small salad

Steamed green beans

Steamed parsnips

Sesame seed butter

Shavegrass tea

Gelatin dessert

CHAPTER 10

HOW TO HELP OVERWEIGHT CHILDREN

I n recent years, the problem of overweight in children—including newborns—has sur-faced and needs to be taken seriously, since overweight and obesity increase health risks for asthma, cardiovascular disease, and possibly diabetes among children. Lack of adequate dietary advice to pregnant mothers may allow out-of-control eating, which affects the fetus and leads to a newborn with a higher than normal amount of fat in body tissues. Overweight in chil-dren of any age, if not acknowledged and taken care of, may be carried into adulthood and lead to serious health problems as well as low self-esteem. If one or both parents are over-weight or obese, the probability is higher that some or all of their children will be overweight or obese, in part because of parent modeling and a dietary context that favors overeating.

Studies have shown that bottle-fed babies are more likely to have overweight problems than babies that are breast-fed. Breast-fed babies stop feeding when they are full, while mothers of bottle-fed babies often try to get the baby to drink the whole bottle of milk. This is an early form of the "eat-everything-on-your-plate" syndrome, which encourages overeating. Although there is evidence for genetic-based over-weight and specific health conditions that cause overweight, the overwhelming cause for overweight and obesity is overeat-ing and a lifestyle that supports overweight or obesity.

The best chance of catching and correcting overweight problems is while children are young and more easily cor-rectable. Healthy, normal-weight children most often grow up to be healthy, normal-weight adults.

We find that at birth the normal infant's body starts out with 12 percent fat, and by six months of age it has developed a total of 25 percent fat. This gradually diminishes to 15 to 18 percent as children approach puberty (nine to sixteen years for girls, thirteen to fifteen years for boys). At puberty, the fat per-centage in boys holds steady while girls increase in body fat. By the time girls are eighteen years old, their bodies contain 20 to 25 percent fatty tissue, but the boys still have 15 to 18 percent. As boys and girls grow into young adults, their body fat reaches 30 to 40 percent of their total weight, lower if they exercise regularly. Body fat normally increases through the adult years, doubling in men from age twenty to age fifty and going up by 50 percent in women over the same age range.

The central issue in weight and amount of body fat is whether the calories ingested in food from day to day are more or less equal to the calories expended in the body's internal functions plus the calories spent in physical activities. In the United States, the rise in the prevalence of overweight and obesity in adults over the past few decades has been traced to food and lifestyle habits that began in childhood, in which intake of food calories has exceeded the burning of calories through normal metabolism plus life activities. (We can put this another way by saying that food energy input exceeds food energy output.) This has prompted researchers to have a look at our current generation of youngsters and compare overweight statistics from prior decades with today's statistics.

In the 1990s, about 25 to 30 percent of U.S. children (aged six to eleven) and adolescents (aged twelve to seventeen) were found to be obese by the National Health Examination Surveys I to III, as compared with 10 to 15 percent prior to 1970. Overweight means a child is up to 20 percent above the mean weight, and severely obese is applied to those 40 percent or more over the mean weight. From 1960 to the 1990s, obesity increased 54 percent in six- to eleven-year-olds and 39 percent in adolescents twelve to seventeen years old. The highest percentages of obesity were found in Hispanic, Native American, and African American children. Since overweight children often become overweight adults, doctors began looking for risk factors for disease among them.

THE BOGALUSA, LOUISIANA, HEART STUDY

Between 1973 and 1994, the Bogalusa Heart Study researchers from the Center for Disease Control and Tulane University conducted seven studies involving over 9,300 children from five to seventeen years old. They found that 58 percent of the overweight schoolchildren, including five- to ten-year-olds, were found to have at least one cardiovascular risk factor. In fact, 20 percent of the overweight kids had two or more cardiovascular risk factors.

When the researchers compared their data on overweight children with data from normal-weight children, they found that the overweight kids were:

2.4 times more likely to have an elevated level of total cholesterol

2.4 times more likely to have elevated diastolic blood pressure

4.5 times more likely to have higher systolic blood pressure

3 times more likely to have adverse levels of low-density cholesterol and adverse levels of high-density cholesterol

7 times more likely to have elevated triglyceride levels

12 times more likely to have high fasting insulin levels

This means it is *very important* to bring children to a normal weight as early in life as possible in order to avoid serious health problems as they grow older. Tobacco use by adolescents introduces another cardiovascular risk factor. Other studies have confirmed additional risk factors.

Obese children are more likely to experience orthopedic problems, such as bowed legs and stress problems in the joints of the hips, knees, and ankles. They are more likely to develop skin problems like heat rash, dermatitis in the fatty folds of the skin, and acne. Depression and low self-esteem are common, and more debilitating psychological problems may develop. Studies have shown evidence of severe prejudice against overweight children by normal-weight children as early as kindergarten.

Many children's hospitals have become aware of the importance of taking overweight seriously and have developed programs to deal with it, including counseling of parents. One easy-to-overlook problem is the amount of fruit juice children drink—which can amount to over a thousand calories a day. Another obvious problem is too much TV, which cuts into the time that children would ordinarily be physically active, burning off calories.

Parents should set a good example by watching their own weight, eating right, and exercising. They can also encourage and praise the child who is keeping to his or her diet and exercise program and reward him or her with gifts (*not food*) and special events like camping out, a trip to the zoo, a movie, the circus, and so forth. Praise, encouragement, and rewards help build and establish good diet and exercise habits. Parents can teach children games that make exercise fun and interesting. Overweight children need more encouragement and stimulation to exercise because it is harder for them, but as they gain skill and confidence, they begin to enjoy sports and exercise more.

TEACHING A CHILD GOOD FOOD HABITS

A balanced diet, such as my Health and Harmony Food Regimen, is the starting point of the child's reducing program. Toddlers are generally taken care of by counting up the usual calorie intake and reducing it by 200 calories per day. Younger children will need a 900 to 1,200 calorie intake, and teenagers will need 1,200 calories. This should be worked out with your doctor.

Foods are divided into three categories—low calorie, average, and high calorie. Low-calorie foods are those 20 calories per serving or less (all vegetables) and are called "green light" or "green" food for go. "Yellow" foods are those for which caution is needed, mostly foods in the middle range of calories in each food group: grains, fruits and vegetables, dairy products, and meat, poultry, and fish. "Red" foods are stop foods, the high-calorie, fat-fried, sugar-saturated, and junk foods.

Parents are in charge, most of the time, of what their children eat and how much is allowable in portion sizes. Mothers, particularly, but fathers, too, can take part in teaching children the *green, yellow,* and *red* foods. With children, as with adults, meals within two or three hours of bedtime should be avoided. We have to realize that teenagers can't be pressured. Let them be responsible for their diets and exercise while setting a good example yourself. Praise them when they do well, encourage them when they forget, but avoid criticism. They simply don't respond to it. Teaching children to choose good foods and healthy activities can begin at age five, in most cases. From ages eight to twelve, most can be taught the "game" of keeping records of their own food intake and exercise activities, but parents should still play a strong leading role.

CHILDREN AND EXERCISE

Many people, children included, find it hard to lose weight by simply eating less. That's why exercise is so important.

Encourage and teach your children activities and exercises they enjoy, and don't persist in trying to get them to do things beyond their level of skill or ability. Start easy and work them up to harder activities. Do exercises with them. Take walks, play catch, go swimming. They will do things with you they won't do by themselves. Take them to playgrounds and pay attention to them as they climb on the monkey bars, slide down the slides, and use the various items of play equipment. An adult's attention is a strong motivating factor in what and how much children will do. As they gain in skill and self-confidence in sports like skating, soccer, softball, and others, they will begin doing more on their own, increasing in motivation.

BUILD A BETTER ATTITUDE

We do not try to treat obesity because obesity is only a symptom. Our goal is to build toward a healthy lifestyle, so that the whole body will be taken care of. Avoid teaching your child to focus on overweight as a problem, and instead teach him or her to have the healthiest body possible. Have a positive attitude and encourage a positive attitude in your children. When we teach children the value of a healthy body and how to make a healthy body, the weight problem is automatically taken care of in time.

CHAPTER 11

GOOD DIETS AND BAD DIETS

Many popular magazines and tabloids print the diets that famous TV and movie stars use to lose weight, telling the reader, "You, too, can shed unwanted ugly fat and look stunning by following the diets of the stars." Are these diets any good? Let's take a look.

First, we have to realize that the reason so many diet articles are being published is because everyone is looking for an easy, attractive, fast weight-loss diet. Second, the average person tends to believe that the stars' diet foods taste better and work faster than the diets most doctors know about, so many people take the stars' diets very seriously—at least until they've tried three or four of them. We have to realize that stars are not nutrition or diet experts.

Another thing we need to realize is that many of the popular stars lead unusually harsh, grueling lives. They are exposed to fatigue more often than most people, their working schedules are irregular and stressful, and we find that fame and constant media attention take their toll on a person's life. Most TV and movie stars do not live normal lives. Fatigue, stress, public exposure, and fast living all tend to create acid conditions in the body, and this is especially true of the stars. So weight-loss diets that are helpful to the stars may not be helpful to the average person.

IT ISN'T A MATTER OF *WHO* IS RIGHT BUT *WHAT* IS RIGHT

There are gourmet diets that emphasize natural foods. Some people have to stuff mushrooms, braise the endive, or even broil grapefruit. There is nothing wrong with adding a touch of elegance to a natural diet and have more enjoyment as your body molds to better foods.

People respond to diets differently. Some people are built like racehorses. You can feed them all day long and they never put on a pound! The ribs of some of those horses are showing all the time. Other horses eat a little grain and get so fat they are too sluggish to ride. Never follow anyone who says, "I can eat anything and it doesn't bother me." That's how people get into trouble. Let's find out *what* is right and not *who* is right.

I have had a lot of experience with overweight people who have taken off a pound a week by dieting, and in one year, a person can lose about 50 pounds. The wonderful thing about it is that these people developed good bodies, and they were able to keep their weight down by just eating the right foods.

The Weight Watchers' "fun" diet has a lot of good points in it, showing what foods we can have over a period of one day. Of course, they encourage using skim milk, while I would suggest yogurt. I believe whole, natural, pure foods are best for us, and I would not recommend pickles to please anyone. I would rather make sure we stick to the natural as much as possible.

Happiness comes to us when we feel well, but so many people are living a moody life because they aren't using foods that feed the vital organs, glands, and tissues properly. They don't have a good balance of nutrients in the bloodstream. They are one-sided persons; they think one-sided, they act one-sided. Some become double personalities like Dr. Jekyll and Mr. Hyde. We find these conditions are not necessary when we are living right.

Some people diet and exercise so they can have sexier bodies. This isn't going to hurt anybody, but if you are living right, you don't have to worry about your body. A naturally healthy body is a naturally sexy body, the best body you can have. Besides, each body is unique. No two people's minds are the same. No two people's glands are the same. For these reasons, we have to eat according to our individual needs. If somebody could find a diet that would increase sex appeal dramatically, everyone would go on that type of diet. But, in my program, we are going for balance, and the balance has to be measured by nutritional values.

All in all, when you look at so many of the available diets, it is well that we consider the natural and unnatural aspects. We consider the excess or deficiency of calories. We consider whether the food combinations are good or bad. We consider when a person eats during the day, how many meals he has, how many snacks he nibbles between meals. We consider what has prompted the excess eating, what has caused the weight gain in the past. These are all part of my patient's problems, and I could add more. I realize that problems come from bad eating. So what are we going to do first? Are we going to take care of it mentally or physically? We have to take care of it both ways. It's a mental and physical problem.

CHAPTER 12

CONCLUDING THOUGHTS

L et's not fool ourselves. It is not the diet program that loses weight; it is the person who uses the diet program. Your body is designed to operate in accordance with certain natural laws, and only when you live in obedience to those laws, respecting the basic integrity and needs of your body, will you look and feel your very best.

My reducing diet plan avoids the extreme ways. If you follow it diligently and make the changes I have suggested in your lifestyle, you should be able to control your weight without difficulty. Overcoming weight problems requires paying attention to the whole person—body, mind, and spirit—not just the symptom of unsightly bulges in the wrong places. Fat is a symptom that something is wrong in the body or lifestyle, and diets that treat only the symptom will fail. My plan works because we are taking care of the causes of weight and health problems, not the side effects of those causes.

Remember, if you are over fifty years of age or if you have chronic disease, it is an absolute must that you see a doctor and discuss your plans to lose weight with him or her. Reducing diets can be very dangerous when certain ailments are present, such as diabetes, hypoglycemia, and heart disease. Don't take chances. See a doctor and get counseling before beginning your reducing diet.

Overeating is the most obvious cause of obesity, and when overeating is simply due to carelessness in eating habits, the problem can be most easily taken care of. Keep a notebook or diary of what you eat and the times you eat for one month; this will help you adapt to more controlled eating habits. If the overeating is due to unhappiness or boredom, you will need to take a different approach. You may have to resolve a long-standing marriage problem, let go of an old grudge, change jobs, or find more fulfilling activities to break the overeating habit. If the weight problem is due to organic causes, your doctor can help you find the best way to take care of it.

I often recommend several laboratory tests, which can be helpful, and you should consult with your doctor on whether to use them. A thyroid test will show whether your thyroid gland may be contributing to your weight problem. The SMA Panel, complete blood count, and urinalysis provide a good deal of information about your state of health. If there are imbalances or deficiencies, it is best to know. My Health and Harmony Food Regimen will help overcome most imbalances, mineral deficiencies, and other lifestyle-related problems.

Whether the overeating came first or some other problem caused it, the consequent obesity has caused certain imbalances in body chemistry and functions. Reducing may bring about periods of discomfort as organs and tissues throw off old toxins in the process of using up fat and replacing old tissue with new tissue, but these periods do not usually last long if they are natural healing crises or elimination processes. If the discomfort becomes severe or persists, check with your doctor.

Don't allow yourself to become bothered by teasing from relatives. Perhaps you have dieted before and gained it all back. Don't let the family needle you into thinking that's what will happen again. My reducing plan will not result in rebound weight gain if you follow instructions and change to a healthier lifestyle.

Avoid the temptation to lose weight as fast as possible. I realize how satisfying it is to see the bathroom scale show a loss of a pound a day or more, but getting rid of fat that fast generates ketone bodies, fat breakdown products that can damage the liver. And high-protein reducing diets generally result in unassimilated protein breakdown products that can damage the kidneys, whether you are losing weight rapidly or slowly.

Remember, 95 percent of those who resort to rapid weight-loss diets gain all the weight back again, many times with a few extra pounds. Avoid any diet plan or pill when advertisements or labels use words like super, powerful, miraculous, fabulous, sensational, thrilling, exciting, startling, and breakthrough. These are aimed at people who don't know any better. You do now.

Snacking is probably the biggest problem for most overweight people. According to the *Journal of the American Dietetic Association,* 99 percent of Americans snack, and 50 percent of Americans snack several times daily. They snack to satisfy cravings, to stop hunger, to relax, to pass the time, or to increase energy. The TV era stimulated vastly increased snacking, while in the 1990s, low-fat snacking became popular. Snacking is now a $42 billion annual business, with up to 25 percent of the daily calories consumed at snacktimes. We find that 40 percent of women and 19 percent of men feel guilty about between-meal snacks. However, feeling guilty doesn't solve the problem. Many snack foods are loaded with chemical additives, fried in hot oil or grease, served with bread, or loaded with sugar.

Fast food is a big contributor to this problem. As Table 12.1 reveals, it is very hard to select a healthy, balanced meal at a fast-food restaurant.

For those who have tried everything and failed to lose weight or keep it off even under a doctor's supervision, surgery may be considered if the danger to health from obesity is great.

Table 12.1. **Selected Fast Foods to Avoid**

Food	Calories
Hot dog	291
Double hamburger	350
Quarter-pounder with cheese	521
French fries	220
Onion rings	341
Apple turnover	290
Chocolate cake	250
Jelly donut	275
Fish, chips, and coleslaw (large)	1,100
Half of 15-inch pizza	1,200
Fried chicken (3 pieces)	660
Chocolate shake	365
Banana split	580
Hot fudge sundae	580
Small fruit sundae	190
Sugared donut	255

Gastric partition, which staples the stomach to leave a smaller pouch for food, may result in a 30 percent weight loss. Small meals must be eaten thereafter. Bypass operations join the stomach to the small intestine so that half the length of the bowel is bypassed. Thirty percent weight loss is common, but there can be serious long-term effects such as diarrhea, bloating, gas, sodium-potassium imbalance, joint pains, skin rash, liver damage, and so on. Usually people over fifty years of age or over 330 pounds in weight are considered too risky for surgery. Liposuction procedures increased by 264 percent from 1992 to 1998, years when overweight and obesity were climbing rapidly. Liposuction is a surgical procedure that can remove fat from the thighs, abdomen, hips, buttocks, knees, arms, chin, cheeks, neck, and so on, but the Mayo Clinic says it is not "a treatment for obesity." Pain, swelling, bleeding, and temporary numbness are experienced by most people who undergo the procedure. Weight gain may recur, usually in parts of the body other than those on which the procedure was performed. It is primarily cosmetic, not a weight-reducing technique.

BEST TIPS FOR SUCCESSFUL WEIGHT REDUCTION

1. Don't think you can lose weight faster by skipping breakfast or lunch. The body metabolism simply slows down and burns fewer calories. Breakfast normalizes blood sugar levels for the day and is very important.
2. If you eat out, have a small salad at home first. Select something from the restaurant menu that is not fried, creamed, battered, or sauteed. Don't order obviously fattening foods of any kind. Think about what you want to eat before going out. Drink water before meals.

3. Serve your children healthy, low-fat meals. Research has shown that young children on a high-fat food routine may grow up into overweight adults even though they do not overeat.

4. Deliberately visualize yourself as slim, wearing smart new clothes, as often as you like. Read fashion magazines. Visit department stores and clothing stores to plan the outfits you'll want to buy when you reach your weight goal.

5. The best way to stop habitual use of a particular food or food group—such as peanuts, corn chips, potato chips, candy, or ice cream—is to stop cold. Don't try to taper off. Don't buy the stuff and don't have it in the house.

6. Dr. Kenneth Cooper, a pioneer in fitness and exercise, recommends having 25 percent of your caloric intake at breakfast, 50 percent at lunch, and 25 percent at dinner. (He coined the term "aerobics" in 1968 and established the Cooper Clinic, a fitness institute near Dallas, Texas.) Heavy meals eaten late in the day or early evening are more likely to turn to fat.

7. Search for low-calorie gourmet treats in delicatessens, supermarkets, and health food stores. Make eating properly more fun.

8. It is often easier—even fun—to lose weight along with one or more other people. Pick a friend who wants to lose weight (or several friends). Encourage one another, share good low-calorie food or meal ideas, and compare notes on how you are doing.

9. Don't take naps after meals, or more of your food intake will turn to fat. Go for a walk if you can. Don't eat your evening meal or any heavy foods later than three hours before bedtime.

10. Whole grain brown rice and millet are the least fattening of the cereal grains and starches. Use them more often than others.

11. Exercise at least one-half hour every morning to increase your rate of calorie burning for the whole day—faster weight loss. Work out to the perspiration point at least twice a week.

12. Eat plenty of high-fiber foods—whole cereal grains, fresh fruits, and vegetables. Use a teaspoon or two of psyllium husks, rice bran, or wheat bran with each low-fiber meal to increase bulk and hasten bowel transit time.

13. Herbal diurectic teas such as KB-11 or Cleavers tea, taken twice a day, help cleanse tissues and prevent excess water retention. To reduce water, you may take these in tablet form.

14. Take one or two beet tablets with each meal for a mild laxative effect and to stimulate the flow of bile from the liver and gallbladder.

15. Avoid all fried or greasy foods, sugar, alcohol, white flour products, and as many processed foods as possible.

16. Think positively about your goals and rehearse them often. Put a meaning to your efforts.

17. Eliminate table salt, or, if you must have it, use a little evaporated sea salt. Use vegetable substitutes or broth from the health food store.

18. Take one or two Novia Scotia dulse tablets with each meal, or sprinkle soups, salads, and other foods liberally with dulse powder. Kelp can be used in the same way.

19. Face and take care of any personal problems, boredom, or depression that encourages you to overeat. Psychosomatic problems may be helped by counseling.

20. You may want to try 100 milligrams of niacin per meal and work up gradually (50 milligrams per week) to 1,000

milligrams per meal to flush the surface blood capillaries at the extremities and carry away toxic materials and fatty breakdown products. *Always take after a meal.*

21. Use plenty of raw foods—60 percent of your daily food intake, at least.

22. Realize that it is all right to be hungry and skip a meal.

23. Don't eat meals by the clock—wait until you are hungry.

24. A sauna or steam bath twice a week to the point of perspiration will help. Don't drink plain water afterward, but use a teaspoon of broth powder in the water so that the potassium will prevent excess water absorption.

25. If you use your credit card to charge fattening meals, get rid of the card.

26. Eat slowly—put your knife and fork down between bites to give yourself time to feel full before you overeat. Remember, it is okay to stop eating before you feel full.

27. Thiamine, a B-complex vitamin that helps convert food to energy, may assist weight loss. Cod liver oil (two capsules a day) and vitamin C will help support the immune system as you lose weight.

28. Drink at least two quarts of water (eight 8-ounce glasses) every day, more on hot days. Dehydration—even at low levels—favors weight gain, according to Dr. F. Batmanghelidj.

Remember, a permanent change to a more natural lifestyle is the key to permanent weight control without dieting once you have reached the weight that is natural to your height and body frame. Good nutrition, adequate exercise and rest, positive thinking, good friends and relationships, loving yourself, a fulfilling occupation and home life—all these contribute importantly to your well-being and to stabilized weight.

INDEX

Tables are indicated with an italic *t*.